The MACAT Library
世界思想宝库钥匙丛书

解析西蒙娜·德·波伏娃

《第二性》

AN ANALYSIS OF
SIMONE DE BEAUVOIR'S
THE SECOND SEX

Rachele Dini ◎ 著

杨建玫 ◎ 译

上海外语教育出版社
外教社 SHANGHAI FOREIGN LANGUAGE EDUCATION PRESS

目　录

引 言 ⋯⋯⋯⋯⋯⋯⋯⋯⋯⋯⋯⋯⋯⋯⋯⋯⋯⋯⋯⋯⋯⋯ 1

　西蒙娜·德·波伏娃其人　　　　　　　　　　2

　《第二性》的主要内容　　　　　　　　　　　3

　《第二性》的学术价值　　　　　　　　　　　4

第一部分：学术渊源　⋯⋯⋯⋯⋯⋯⋯⋯⋯⋯⋯⋯　7

　1. 作者生平与历史背景　　　　　　　　　　8

　2. 学术背景　　　　　　　　　　　　　　　12

　3. 主导命题　　　　　　　　　　　　　　　17

　4. 作者贡献　　　　　　　　　　　　　　　22

第二部分：学术思想　⋯⋯⋯⋯⋯⋯⋯⋯⋯⋯⋯　27

　5. 思想主脉　　　　　　　　　　　　　　　28

　6. 思想支脉　　　　　　　　　　　　　　　33

　7. 历史成就　　　　　　　　　　　　　　　38

　8. 著作地位　　　　　　　　　　　　　　　43

第三部分：学术影响　⋯⋯⋯⋯⋯⋯⋯⋯⋯⋯⋯　49

　9. 最初反响　　　　　　　　　　　　　　　50

　10. 后续争议　　　　　　　　　　　　　　56

　11. 当代印迹　　　　　　　　　　　　　　61

　12. 未来展望　　　　　　　　　　　　　　66

术语表 ⋯⋯⋯⋯⋯⋯⋯⋯⋯⋯⋯⋯⋯⋯⋯⋯⋯⋯⋯⋯ 71

人名表 ⋯⋯⋯⋯⋯⋯⋯⋯⋯⋯⋯⋯⋯⋯⋯⋯⋯⋯⋯⋯ 78

CONTENTS

WAYS IN TO THE TEXT 87

    Who Was Simone de Beauvoir?   88

    What Does *The Second Sex* Say?   89

    Why Does *The Second Sex* Matter?   91

SECTION 1: INFLUENCES 93

    Module 1: The Author and the Historical Context   94

    Module 2: Academic Context   99

    Module 3: The Problem   105

    Module 4: The Author's Contribution   110

SECTION 2: IDEAS 115

    Module 5: Main Ideas   116

    Module 6: Secondary Ideas   122

    Module 7: Achievement   127

    Module 8: Place in the Author's Work   132

SECTION 3: IMPACT 139

    Module 9: The First Responses   140

    Module 10: The Evolving Debate   146

    Module 11: Impact and Influence Today   151

    Module 12: Where Next?   156

Glossary of Terms 161

People Mentioned in the Text 168

Works Cited 174

引言

要 点

- 西蒙娜·德·波伏娃是法国激进的哲学家和作家。
- 《第二性》分析女人为何一直比男人拥有更少的权力和自由。
- 德·波伏娃运用多个学科来论证妇女在整个历史长河中始终遭受压迫的境况。其著作推动了女权主义*运动的开展。

西蒙娜·德·波伏娃其人

西蒙娜·德·波伏娃是法国激进的哲学家、作家和政治活动家。她的开创性著作关注妇女的劣势地位，推动了女权运动的产生。

德·波伏娃生于 1908 年，在巴黎的一个中产阶级家庭长大，是一位才华横溢的学者。她的父亲是一位律师，总是鼓励她学习。她的母亲是一位虔诚的罗马天主教徒。在女修道院学校学习时，德·波伏娃曾考虑过做一名修女，但是后来她成为一位终身的无神论者。

1929 年，德·波伏娃获得了巴黎索邦大学（也被称为巴黎大学）的哲学*学位，成为当时为数不多的女大学毕业生之一。21 岁时，她在著名的巴黎高等师范学院遇见了哲学家让-保罗·萨特*。直到 1980 年萨特去世，他们一直保持着恋人兼朋友的关系。德·波伏娃后来成为一名中学教师，但是她和萨特涉嫌在 1939 年诱奸她的一名女学生，她也因卷入这起诉讼丑闻而被停职。

德·波伏娃于 1943 年出版了第一部小说《女宾》（基于自己的丑闻创作而成），次年发表了第一篇哲学散文《皮鲁斯与斯内阿斯》。接着她出版了《模糊伦理学》（1947）和《第二性》（1949）。

1954 年，她的半自传体小说《名士风流》问世。[1]

1972 年，德·波伏娃宣称自己是女权主义者，修正了她先前的"社会主义革命*足以解放*妇女"的立场。[2]1986 年，她因肺炎去世，葬于巴黎蒙帕纳斯公墓萨特的墓旁。

《第二性》的主要内容

德·波伏娃的著作论述了自人类文明伊始至今妇女的社会地位。其中心论点是，自古以来妇女就被迫从属于男性，整个人类境况都由男性的思维来审视，由男性的话语来描述，而妇女处于失语的状态。

德·波伏娃运用三个理论框架来证明自己的观点。第一个是历史唯物主义*，该理论强调社会、经济条件以及阶级对历史形成的影响。德·波伏娃还运用存在主义*的观点进行论证，该哲学体系强调在上帝或其他超自然力量缺失的世界中个人的自由和选择。后来，她运用精神分析学*来论证人类行为的根本（即"潜意识"）原因。

德·波伏娃的历史唯物主义研究揭示了女人在其生活的每个领域是怎样陷入依赖男人的境况的，这种境况导致她们在文化或社会中没有真正的权力。她强调社会如何像对待孩子那样把女人当作法律上的未成年人来对待，这种方法限制了女人与男人平等参与公共生活的能力。由于这些原因，女人在重大的历史事件中大多处于缺失的状态，而男人始终在经济、政治和社会上被赋予更多的权力，所以能够对文化和历史事件产生更大的影响。[3]

德·波伏娃通过存在主义视角审视女性的命运，提出女性气质是被建构的。这里她是指人的本性受外界因素的影响，该观点与"人的本性是天生注定的"这一传统哲学观点背道而驰。作为一位存在主义者，德·波伏娃认为，人天生并不具有任何特定的价值观，其身份只由生活环境塑造。《第二性》的一个著名观点是：女人不是天生的，而是由养育方式和社会环境造就的。

德·波伏娃认为，纵观历史，女人一直扮演着"他者"*的角色。"他者"是一个哲学术语，指与人的自我相分离或者有很大差别。德·波伏娃提出，女人之所以被社会视为"他者"，是因为她们只被视为男人的附属品。她们被当作男人欲望的客体、其后嗣的母亲或者照顾其他人的人。男人从自己的视角否认女人的自我主体性（指自视为独立个体的权利），这是去人性化的*，也剥夺了女人的权力。

在《第二性》中，德·波伏娃运用精神分析学揭露了神话*中有关女性气质的矛盾和不真实性，这些女性特质遍布于艺术、文学、宗教和通俗文化中。德·波伏娃指出，有关女性气质的文化理解毫无事实依据。相反，它们源于男性的恐惧和欲望，表达了男人想在世界上拥有、独占和取胜的欲望。女人在社会上的唯一目的就是满足男人的这些欲望。在这些神话中，女人的角色都很顺从被动。没有男人追求、引诱她们或者娶她们为妻，女人就没有存在的理由。

《第二性》的学术价值

《第二性》是女性社会经历相关研究的里程碑。有人认为它标志着女权主义的诞生。德·波伏娃令人瞩目的成就在于她揭示了现代社会广泛存在的性别歧视*现象。她以开阔的视野，有条不紊地运用数个学科的批判性方法开展研究，这使得她的论述横跨文学、文化和学术领域。

德·波伏娃着重论述了几个世纪以来广为接受的与妇女的家庭地位以及婚姻的功能相关的观念，并对有关女性气质的观点提出质疑。1949 年，在保守的法国，《第二性》引起了激烈的争议，而德·波伏娃也因其观点和私生活饱受批评和嘲讽。然而，《第二性》却激起了人们对父权制 *（以男性为中心）立场的争论，而且这些争论几十年不绝于耳，持续至今。

确实，对于 21 世纪的读者而言，德·波伏娃的许多理论好像是在陈述明显的事实。像《第二性》这种激进的著作所提出的观点，常常难逃被后人认为已经落伍的厄运。但是，通过质疑原来的状况，该书促进了妇女境况的改变。该书的部分内容已经过时 *，则可以说明德·波伏娃的愿望得到了实现。这就意味着人们会觉得德·波伏娃分析的某些方面已经过时，而她的一些诉求（例如，她呼吁所有的妇女出去工作）可能已经被有关妇女如何能够既工作又抚养孩子的问题所取代。

同时，从整体而言，德·波伏娃的著作仍与如今人们争论的热点紧密相关。人们之所以仍在查阅《第二性》，是因为它对学界和社会所关心的核心领域作出了贡献，比如她着重论述了男性的权力在文化神话 *中是怎样被构建的。而社会给女孩灌输有关女性气质的信息这个问题，在波伏娃首次将其指出后的半个多世纪里，仍是人们关注的焦点。

对于我们怎样界定性别和性取向的问题，该书所提出的方法仍然具有高度的独创性。该书的历史重要性也是独一无二的。它为女权主义运动铺平了道路，有助于在法国、美国乃至整个世界发起为妇女争取权利的斗争。

1. 西蒙娜·德·波伏娃:《女宾》,罗杰·森豪斯和伊冯·莫伊斯译,纽约:诺顿公司,1954 年;《皮鲁斯与斯内阿斯》,巴黎:伽利玛出版社,1944 年;《模糊伦理学》,伯纳德·弗里希特曼译,纽约:德尔出版社,1996 年;《名士风流》,伦纳德·M.弗里德曼译,纽约:诺顿公司,1991 年。

2. 伊丽莎白·法莱兹:《西蒙娜·德·波伏娃:批判性读物》,伦敦:劳特利奇出版社,1998 年,第 6 页。

3. 西蒙娜·德·波伏娃:《第二性》,H. M. 帕什利译,纽约:阿尔弗雷德·A.克诺夫出版社,1953 年,第 123 页。

第一部分：学术渊源

1 作者生平与历史背景

要点 🔑

- 《第二性》成书于第二次世界大战 * 之后，是一部论述从古至今妇女所受压迫的开山之作。

- 德·波伏娃所处的学术环境和她的伴侣、哲学家让-保罗·萨特都对该著作的成形起到了重要作用。

- 反殖民主义 * 运动、美国民权运动 *、战后有关反犹太主义 * 的讨论以及法国就业女性最近的收益状况都对她产生了影响。

为何要读这部著作？

西蒙娜·德·波伏娃的《第二性》于 1949 年首次出版，被视为划时代的女权主义宣言。她史无前例地剖析了历史上妇女的地位，引发了长达几十年有关性别歧视如何支配妇女的讨论。

德·波伏娃运用一系列理论方法探讨了妇女受压迫的根源及广泛影响，因而该书成为女权运动 * 的一个关键文本。如今我们承认妇女是劳动力的重要组成部分，并接受部分妇女不想要孩子的现实，这些在一定程度上都得益于《第二性》。

人的性别身份并非生而有之，而是受社会和文化的影响获得的——德·波伏娃是第一位提出这种观点的思想家，而这一观点对酷儿理论 * 和性别研究 * 至关重要。德·波伏娃提出："女人不是天生的，而是后天造就的"，这是女权主义理论中最著名的论断。[1]

《第二性》采用跨学科 * 的方法探讨了文化神话的力量以及有关女性气质的思想如何影响了孩童的发展。该书是一部不朽的学术著作，对当今有关妇女地位的争论仍然重要。

> "女人是什么？……我提出这个问题的这一举动本身就很重要。男人从来不会想要写一部关于男人特别状况的著作。但是，如果我想要界定我自己的话，我必须首先说：'我是个女人。'所有进一步的探讨必须以此事实为基础。"
>
> —— 西蒙娜·德·波伏娃：《第二性》

作者生平

西蒙娜·德·波伏娃于 1908 年出生在巴黎一个富裕的中产阶级家庭。虽然她在罗马天主教 * 的环境中成长，但是她在 14 岁时成为一位无神论者。德·波伏娃成绩优异，于 1929 年毕业于巴黎著名的索邦大学，获得哲学学位，是该校当年仅有的九名女毕业生之一。

大学毕业后，德·波伏娃在享有盛誉的专门培养学者和公务员的巴黎高等师范学院旁听学习，尽管当时该校还从未接收过任何一名女性。就是在这里，21 岁的她遇到了同为哲学家的让-保罗·萨特。毕业后，她到法国鲁昂市的一所中学任教，并和萨特成为伴侣。德·波伏娃反对婚姻，他们终身没有生育。他们的开放式关系在当时颇受非议。当波伏娃被指控对一名女学生有不端性行为时，丑闻也随之爆发。这位学生的家长指控德·波伏娃和萨特在 1939 年共同诱奸了他们 17 岁的女儿。

这些指控在事件发生后许久才被提出，导致德·波伏娃在 1943 年被学校辞退。她的第一部小说《女宾》（1943）就是在这一事件的基础上虚构而成的。她在 1944 年发表了第一篇哲学性散文《皮鲁斯与斯内阿斯》，在 1947 年出版了《模糊伦理学》，在 1949

年出版了《第二性》。而 1954 年出版的小说《名士风流》还获得了法国最高文学奖——龚古尔文学奖。

德·波伏娃晚年时撰写了一些游记散文和一部四卷本的自传。1972 年，她第一次声明自己是女权主义者，修正了她早期所提出的"社会主义革命将足以解放妇女"的观点。[2] 她在法国和美国参加争取妇女权利的政治运动，直至 1986 年去世。

创作背景

德·波伏娃的著作受到了第二次世界大战以及激进观点的影响。这些观点还催生了许多迥异的思想和运动，包括马克思主义 *、存在主义和民权运动。

马克思主义是基于 19 世纪的哲学家和社会主义理论家卡尔·马克思 * 的著作而形成的一种政治理论。马克思认为，资本主义 * 经济体系因追求利润而导致阶级不平等，并且鼓励对劳动力进行剥削。德·波伏娃还受到苏联 * 马克思主义思想的影响。苏联领袖约瑟夫·斯大林 * 推行中央集权的计划经济体制，他声称这种体制通过将所有资源国有化来消除社会阶层差异和私有财产。

在包括德·波伏娃在内的法国左派中，有许多人认为社会主义革命是解决战后法国经济困境的关键途径。在考察新苏维埃妇女所起的作用之后，德·波伏娃形成了自己有关女性自由的观点。

存在主义是一场哲学运动，20 世纪 40 年代由德·波伏娃的伴侣萨特发扬光大。这一哲学理论强调个人的存在以及选择的自由。在《存在主义是一种人道主义》(1946) 中，萨特颠覆了"人生而具有某种身份"的传统观点。相反，他提出："存在先于本质"，"人首先存在着，遇见其自身，在这个世界上活动——然后开始界定自己。"[3]

他的意思是人的身份并非生而有之，而是环境的产物。德·波伏娃认为，如果身份是由社会构建的，那么女性气质同样如此。

德·波伏娃相信，可以利用存在主义思想来解放妇女。当男人去参加第二次世界大战，更多的妇女加入劳动大军之后，法国才在1944年赋予妇女投票权。在《第二性》中，德·波伏娃的一个关注点便是加强并发展妇女在战争期间获得的各种权力。

德·波伏娃的著作也受到了法国反殖民主义运动[4]的影响，该运动为结束法国少数族裔所遭受的压迫而战。1947年的马达加斯加起义*引起了公众对法国殖民地人民遭受压迫的关注。在《第二性》中，德·波伏娃把少数族裔反抗压迫者的团结感与妇女对其压迫者的态度进行对比，并指出这些妇女其实与其压迫者沆瀣一气。她看到，女人与其父亲和丈夫相处得比与其他女人相处得更加和谐。德·波伏娃提出，如果她们想要改变这种状况，就必须转换她们所忠诚的对象，与其他女人团结起来。按照她的观点，如果女人们不团结起来，为妇女自由而战的斗争将会失败。

1. 西蒙娜·德·波伏娃：《第二性》，H. M. 帕什利译，纽约：艾尔弗雷德·A.克诺夫出版社，1953年，第249页。

2. 伊丽莎白·法莱兹：《西蒙娜·德·波伏娃：批判性读物》，伦敦：劳特利奇出版社，1998年，第6页。

3. 让–保罗·萨特："存在主义与人道主义"，《让–保罗·萨特：基础写作》，史蒂芬·普里斯特编，纽约：劳特利奇出版社，2002年，第28页。

4. 玛格丽特·A.西蒙斯：《德·波伏娃和〈第二性〉：女权主义、种族与存在主义的起源》，纽约：罗曼和利特菲尔德出版社，1999年。

2 学术背景

要点 🗝

- 《第二性》并未局限于一个单一的学术领域，德·波伏娃在书中借鉴了历史、哲学和文学的有益成分。

- 该书探讨了人类自由的问题和社会结构在带来自由或压迫方面所起的作用。

- 德·波伏娃利用存在主义的人道主义 *、马克思主义、历史唯物主义和拉康的精神分析理论 * 中的要素来构建其关于女性角色的理论。

著作语境

在《第二性》中，西蒙娜·德·波伏娃采用宽泛的跨学科方法，借鉴哲学、历史和文学批评 * 进行论述。她有必要这样做，因为一个女人的一生并不只限于其性行为、生物特性和经济地位。德·波伏娃在书中谈到，"'阴蒂'和'阴道'这种分类就如'资产阶级' * 和'无产阶级' * 的分类一样，不足以概括一个具体的女人。"[1]

德·波伏娃的著作具有很强的独创性。在 1949 年《第二性》出版之前，几乎没有著作对妇女在历史、文化和社会上的境况进行审视。讨论妇女境况的学者普遍被忽视，直到 20 世纪 70 年代才被女权主义学者从默默无闻中重新发现。这些被忽视的思想家包括哲学家玛莉·渥斯顿克雷福特 *、社会主义作家奥古斯特·倍倍尔 *、人类学家 * 约翰·雅各布·巴霍芬 * 和刘易斯·亨利·摩根 *。

渥斯顿克雷福特在 1792 年发表的《为女权辩护》一书中，主张女人应该像男人一样接受教育。之后，倍倍尔、巴霍芬和摩根专门论述了妇女更为广泛的社会角色，但是在 20 世纪 70 年代中期女权主义学者出现以后，他们的贡献才被承认。[2] 摩根和巴霍芬认为，史前和早期近代社会都是基于母系 * 血缘建立的，这就意味着人们是根据与其母亲的关系来确定身份的。可是，这一观点并未引起人们的关注。[3]

20 世纪 60 年代以前，除了历史系的学者以外，很少有人文学科的学者探讨妇女的地位问题，而英国小说家弗吉尼亚·伍尔芙 * 是一个明显的例外。在她的随笔《一间自己的房间》（1929）里，伍尔芙提出，莎士比亚 * 之所以能成功不仅是因为他的才干，还因为他作为男人所拥有的自由。[4] 但是，就像她之前的倍倍尔和德国哲学家、政治理论家弗里德里希·恩格斯 * 一样，她的观点并未能改变公众对妇女的观念。

> "整个妇女史是由男人创造的，就如同在美国没有黑人问题而有白人问题一样，也如同反犹太主义并非犹太人 * 的问题，而是我们的问题一样；所以女人的问题一直都是男人的问题。"
>
> —— 西蒙娜·德·波伏娃：《第二性》

学科概览

德·波伏娃有关妇女受压迫的历史性分析主要借鉴了马克思主义的历史唯物主义方法。这种分析历史的方法是由政治理论家卡尔·马克思和弗里德里希·恩格斯提出的，主要关注阶级斗争、社会不平等和剥削劳动力的影响。恩格斯通过历史唯物主义的视角看到了妇女在社会中的角色。恩格斯认为，在整个人类历史上，妇女一直都是被交换的客体（即商品），而资本主义意识形态强化了这一点——这一观点启发了德·波伏娃。恩格斯把婚姻看作新娘的父亲和新郎之间进行的一系列金钱交易。相似地，德·波伏娃的主要观点以倍倍尔在《妇女与社会主义》*中的观点为基础，那就是女人"生来就是服役的，在男人面前只是奴隶"。[5]

虽然恩格斯和倍倍尔认为妇女的解放——从压迫下获得自由——有助于社会主义革命的实现，但是德·波伏娃颠覆了这种观点。在她看来，社会主义革命能够解放妇女："我们很容易设想一个男女平等的世界，因为那正是苏维埃革命所承诺的。"[6]换句话说，恩格斯和马克思把妇女当作革命的工具，而德·波伏娃则把革命当作妇女解放的工具。但是，她也认为，历史唯物主义解释妇女经历的能力受到其唯物主义中心点的限制，而该中心点"只不过是把男女简化为经济单位而已"。[7]

德·波伏娃采用与精神分析学的一个分支截然相反的方法发展了她的观点。这一分支由法国人雅克·拉康*发展而来，是一套主要用于理解内心的理论和治疗体系。拉康的"镜像阶段"概念认为，当婴儿认出镜中的映像是自己时，他们就学会视自己为一个完整的个体。但是，德·波伏娃认为对于女童而言并非如此，因为她们从小就受到教导，要按照他人希望的方式来表现和行动。当女孩照镜子时，她看到的并不是自己，而只是外界所期望的她的形象的投射，其中包括通过"把她自己比作公主和仙女"，使自己"看起来像一幅画"。[8]

德·波伏娃也对精神分析学的阳具妒羡理论*提出了挑战。该

14

理论认为，女孩从童年转化为成年的标志是她们在青春期时意识到自己没有阴茎。德·波伏娃把这一理论视为另一种男性观点，她提出："这些理论本身就应该受到精神分析学的研究。"[9]

学术渊源

德·波伏娃利用存在主义哲学来阐释女性受压迫的境况，这填补了历史唯物主义理论和精神分析理论留下的空白。她认为，存在主义的方法考虑到了女人的"整体处境"，女人是"在一个充满价值观的世界中寻找价值观的人"。[10]换句话说，女人不只是一个躯体或者一个经济单位。

《第二性》的中心论点是，女人被看作客体，而男人通过这些客体去了解世界。德·波伏娃运用存在主义的术语来构建这一论点。存在主义认为，人有能力塑造自己的命运，并且可以用自己的条件来界定自己。德·波伏娃发展了这一观点，她认为女人有能力摆脱其次要地位，并能独立地界定自己，不受男人的影响。在她的自传中，德·波伏娃将这一观点归功于萨特，认为他激发了她的灵感，但是，学者们并不认可萨特所起的作用。[11]

该书也借鉴了18世纪德国哲学家格奥尔格·威廉·弗里德里希·黑格尔＊著作中的观点。黑格尔将人的境况描述为"主体"（人）和"他者"（不同于人或与人疏离的存在）的辩证统一。德·波伏娃认为，社会完全按照男人的标准来看待人类，所以把女人降格到"他者"的角色。于是，女人被界定为在社会上和性方面与男人有关，而在行为方式上与男人不同（即"他者"）："女人……发现自己生活在一个男人强迫她具有他者身份的世界中。"[12]

德·波伏娃运用黑格尔的辩证法＊——即把看似矛盾的观点放

在一起，以达到更高层次的真理——来显示女性身份是被消极地构建的。作为人类，我们通过自身来感知世界，所以我们认为自己很重要。但是，社会却让女人认为她们是无关紧要的。她说道："女人人生的戏剧性就在于每个主体（自我）的愿望——她一直认为自己至关重要——和使她变得无关紧要的强制状态之间的矛盾。"[13]女人之所以被视为低人一等，仅仅是因为她们不是男人，而这也是社会把女人当作男人的消极变体来对待的原因。

---

1. 西蒙娜·德·波伏娃：《第二性》，H. M. 帕什利译，纽约：艾尔弗雷德·A. 克诺夫出版社，1953 年，第 91 页。

2. 琼·凯利-加多尔："两性的社会关系：妇女史的方法论意义"，《女权主义与方法论：社会科学问题》，桑德拉·哈丁编，布卢明顿和印第安纳波利斯：印第安纳大学出版社，1987 年，第 22 页。

3. 凯利-加多尔："两性的社会关系"，第 23 页。

4. 弗吉尼亚·伍尔芙：《一间自己的房间》，伦敦和纽约：企鹅出版社，2002 年。

5. 奥古斯特·倍倍尔：《妇女与社会主义》，米塔·斯特恩译，纽约：社会文学公司和合作出版社，1910 年（1879 年）。

6. 德·波伏娃：《第二性》，第 652 页。

7. 德·波伏娃：《第二性》，第 54 页。

8. 德·波伏娃：《第二性》，第 264 页。

9. 德·波伏娃：《第二性》，第 221 页。

10. 德·波伏娃：《第二性》，第 84 页。

11. 爱德华·富布鲁克和凯特·富布鲁克：《性与哲学：对德·波伏娃和萨特的重新思考》，伦敦：布鲁姆斯伯里出版社，2008 年。

12. 德·波伏娃：《第二性》，第 xxviii 页。

13. 德·波伏娃：《第二性》，第 xxviii 页。

3 主导命题

要点 🔑

- 《第二性》呼吁学者和公众行动起来，重新思考他们对妇女及其在社会上的角色的看法。

- 该书质疑精神分析学、哲学和历史中根深蒂固的观点，提出了一个全新的问题：女性遭受压迫的原因和后果是什么？

- 德·波伏娃公开对女性的性行为表现出兴趣，这在当时是不同寻常的事情，而且她本人不合世俗的性生活也招致一些针对她个人的批评。

核心问题

德·波伏娃并非为了回应已有的争论才撰写《第二性》，而是为了开展一项全新的调查。她还提出了重大的问题：女人是什么？当我们谈及人类（humanity）时，为什么总是说"男人"（mankind有"人类"之意）？

德·波伏娃想要探讨社会对性别的确切定义，这就意味着从总体上审视妇女在家庭、工作、政治和文化中的从属地位及其深远的影响。她对女性性行为和生殖的看法明显与当时的心理学家 * 和社会学家 * 的观点背道而驰，而她有关女性主体性（作为一个个体的自由）的观点对于哲学而言则是全新的。

德·波伏娃相信，女人应该在学术研究方面充分发挥作用。她深信，只允许占人类一半数量的男性去研究人文科学的话，轻则对人类产生理解的偏差，重则对人类产生严重的误解。

在《第二性》中，德·波伏娃对社会、心理和生物层面上有关女人的固有观念进行了系统性的质疑和反驳。她甚至对科学家有关女性身体（包括生殖系统和性欲）的假设提出质疑。由此，她向学者和社会大众提出了一系列全新的问题："一个人在女人的生活状态下怎样取得成功？对她而言哪条路行得通，哪条路行不通？在依附的状态下，她怎样才能恢复独立性？"[1]

> "女人不是天生的，而是后天造就的。并非生物的、心理的或经济的命运决定了女性在社会上所展现的角色，而是整个文明造就了这种生物，她介于男性和太监之间，被描述为具有女性气质。只有其他人的干预才能将一个个体塑造成他者。"
>
> —— 西蒙娜·德·波伏娃：《第二性》

参与者

《第二性》对精神分析学、哲学和历史领域约定俗成的观点提出了质疑。首先，德·波伏娃提出，女人面临的挑战并非像精神分析学所断言的那样来自女人内部，而是来自外部，她实现自我的最大障碍存在于文化和社会环境中。"精神分析学提出，一个人的戏剧性人生由他自身展开……但是，一个人的人生是和世界相关的，一个人通过他周围的世界来作出选择，从而界定自我。因此，我们必须转向这个世界去寻找答案。"[2]

其次，德·波伏娃并不相信，一个女人的命运从孩童时代起就已经被规划完毕。精神分析学重点强调人的早期经历和创伤记忆，认为我们难以摆脱这两者的影响。同时，历史唯物主义提出，我们的人生之路由经济条件决定。德·波伏娃虽然承认这些因素的影响，但是她认为女人有能力克服它们。这种观点建立在存在主义的"自由意志"观念上。"为了解释女人的局限性，必须援引她们的处境，而不是她们神秘的本质；因此，未来仍然具有很大的探讨空间。"[3]

最后，德·波伏娃对精神分析学家把女性的心理成熟与其身体联系起来的习惯提出了质疑。例如，精神分析学家认为阴蒂的（而非阴道的）高潮是性不成熟的迹象，而德·波伏娃对该观点表示质疑。[4] 她将这一观点与以下事实联系在一起：阴蒂高潮在没有男人的情况下也会出现，在这种情况下女人没有繁殖功能，而阴道高潮"则把女人打发给男人来处置，要其生育后代……使女人处于依赖男人和种族繁衍的状态。"[5] 德·波伏娃认为，精神分析学把阴蒂高潮诊断为"未成年的"行为，不过是在竭力控制女性的性行为。[6]

当时的论战

在德·波伏娃的同辈中很少有人对妇女受压迫的问题感兴趣，而《第二性》借鉴了老一代作家和思想家的著作，包括马克思主义历史学家奥古斯特·倍倍尔和弗里德里希·恩格斯等人，他们把妇女解放看作社会主义成功的关键。德·波伏娃的著作把这些先前被忽视的关于在资本主义制度中妇女受压迫的观点和她那个时代的政治关注点结合了起来。

在德·波伏娃的同辈中，唯一一个赞成其观点的思想家便是她的伴侣让-保罗·萨特。像德·波伏娃一样，萨特对妇女受压迫的研究兴趣来源于有关社会异化*的马克思主义和存在主义的阐释，社会异化就是将某些人边缘化的过程，其中阶级、财富、种族和宗教都起到了一定的作用。萨特撰写的与压迫有关的著作包括《反犹太主义和犹太人》（1946）以及《孤儿日记》（1948），前者与犹太人受迫害相关，后者讨论了法国黑人文化认同 * 运动中黑人知识分子的反殖民主义诗歌。[7]

第二次世界大战之后，如同法国政治左派的许多人一样，德·波伏娃尤其关注人权和社会平等问题。然而，她在《第二性》中尖锐地批评左派不像重视解放法国殖民地和犹太人那般重视解放妇女。

美国性学家 * 阿尔弗雷德·金赛 * 和德·波伏娃都关注女性性行为的本质，但是金赛却公开批评《第二性》，认为它对提升公众对性行为的理解作用有限。[8]公众对金赛的印象和对德·波伏娃的印象相似。金赛也使不习惯于公开谈论性的保守社会产生了强烈的好奇心和愤怒。

金赛的著作《男性中的性行为》（1948）和《女性中的性行为》（1953）在美国备受关注。[9]德·波伏娃和金赛都因另类的性生活（金赛与他的研究对象发生性行为）而遭到社会的公开批评，[10]甚至有人利用有关其私生活的争议来诋毁他们的著作。金赛和他的研究对象发生性行为被看作对权力的滥用。而德·波伏娃劝说她的一些年轻学生与萨特上床，则被看作不正当的行为。后来，也有人批评说，那是她讨好萨特的一种谄媚方式，而这种方式与她的女权主义观点相矛盾。[11]

---

1. 西蒙娜·德·波伏娃：《第二性》，H. M. 帕什利译，纽约：艾尔弗雷德·A. 克

20

诺夫出版社，1953 年，第 xxix 页。

2. 德·波伏娃：《第二性》，第 44 页。

3. 德·波伏娃：《第二性》，第 672 页。

4. 德·波伏娃：《第二性》，第 71 页。

5. 德·波伏娃：《第二性》，第 71、426 页。

6. 德·波伏娃：《第二性》，第 71、426 页。

7. 让-保罗·萨特：《反犹太主义和犹太人：仇恨根源探析》，乔治·贝克尔译，纽约：司可肯出版社，1948 年；"孤儿日记"，《黑人和马达加斯加法语新诗选》，利奥波德·S.桑格编，巴黎：法兰西大学出版社，1977 年。

8. 沃德尔·鲍尔奥伊：《金赛博士及性研究学会》，康涅狄格州纽黑文：耶鲁大学出版社，1982 年，第 279 页。

9. 阿尔弗雷德·C.金赛等：《男性中的性行为》，布卢明顿：印第安纳大学出版社，1975 年；《女性中的性行为》，布卢明顿：印第安纳大学出版社，1998 年。

10. 詹姆斯·H.琼斯：《阿尔弗雷德·金赛：公共生活/私生活》，纽约：诺顿出版社，1997 年。

11. 约-安·皮拉尔迪："女权主义者解读第二性"，《女权主义解读西蒙娜·德·波伏娃》，玛格丽特·A.西蒙斯编，宾夕法尼亚州立大学帕克分校：宾夕法尼亚州立大学出版社，1995 年，第 40 页。

4 作者贡献

要点

- 西蒙娜·德·波伏娃的《第二性》关注的是古往今来女性受压迫的境况。
- 她对婚姻的批评、对不利于女人的社会和经济因素的分析以及对有关女性气质的神话的披露有助于女权主义运动的开展。
- 《第二性》强调了有关女性的文化神话是怎样深深地根植于文化的所有领域的。

作者目标

西蒙娜·德·波伏娃撰写《第二性》的目的在于充分揭示妇女受压迫的境况，并展示有关女性气质的性别歧视的神话是怎样遍及社会的每个角落的。为此，她把整部书分为两卷，第一卷的题目是《事实和神话》，第二卷的题目是《当今妇女的生活》。

第一卷探讨了女性被征服*（即女性怎样受到控制）的历史。德·波伏娃首先分析了不同学科（包括生物学和心理学）是怎样帮助维持性别的刻板印象的。第二部分展现了在整个人类历史上，妇女怎样被剥夺了"具体的"自由，即实际的权利，如拥有财产或参与政治的权利。德·波伏娃认为，没有具体的自由，女人就无法自视为个体，而女人是"无关紧要的"这一观念阻止了她们要求具体自由的权利。在第一卷的结尾，她聚焦于五位作家的作品中有关女性气质的神话，这五位作家分别是亨利·德·蒙特朗*、D. H. 劳伦斯*、保罗·克洛岱尔*、安德烈·布莱顿*和司汤达*。这些作家的作品都传递了相同的观念："女人心甘情愿地认为（男人）是她的归宿。"[1]

在第二卷中，德·波伏娃转而探讨第一卷论及的观念所带来的持久的遗留问题。她在每一部分探究女人身份的某个阶段（童年时期、青少年时期、婚姻时期、母亲时期）或者文化意义上女性的某个形象（妓女、女同性恋者、单身女人）。德·波伏娃研究了这些阶段和形象，质疑了与其有关的固有观点。例如，在探讨同性恋的章节中，德·波伏娃批评了将女同性恋视为一种发育受阻形式的论断，该观点认为，这一形式是女人性未完全成熟的一种表现。当时有一些心理学家提出，女同性恋只是女人还不成熟、尚未度过青春期的一个迹象[2]。而德·波伏娃则认为，女同性恋其实反映了女人对社会所期望的"女人应当结婚生子"这一观念的抵制："女人的同性恋行为是对调和其自主性*和身体被动性的一种尝试。"简而言之，它是一种女性拒绝被男人征服并为其生育子女的表现形式。[3]

> "（小女孩）所属的历史文化和文学文化、哄她入眠的歌谣和传说，长久以来都带有对男人的褒扬。是男人们建立了希腊、罗马帝国、法兰西和所有其他国家……孩子们所读的书本、神话、小说、传奇都反映了源自男人的傲慢和贪婪的神话。因此，正是透过男人的眼睛，小女孩认识了整个世界，并从中读懂了自己的归宿。"
>
> —— 西蒙娜·德·波伏娃：《第二性》

研究方法

德·波伏娃阐释说，纵观历史，女人一直都是父亲和丈夫所交换的客体。父亲将女儿交给她的丈夫，并以金钱或者土地作为嫁妆*，以补偿其丈夫供养她的费用。而丈夫之所以迎娶新娘，是因为她将为他生儿育女。有工作的女人之所以比男人挣得少，是因为她们的收入只被假定为其丈夫收入的补充。由于这些原因，"男人一直控制并决定着女人的命运，而且并非按照她的兴趣，而是根据他们自己的安排、他们的恐惧和他们的需求。"[4]

德·波伏娃也展示了女孩是如何被教育得想要成为妻子和母亲的。在与布娃娃玩耍的过程中，女孩学着通过布娃娃来建立身份认同："女孩幻想自己被溺爱、被打扮，并按照自己的幻想去溺爱和打扮她的布娃娃；反过来，她自视为一个极美的布娃娃。"[5]女孩明白了这样一个道理："想要取悦别人，她必须使自己'美如一幅画'；于是，她试图把自己打扮得与某一形象相似。"[6]女孩以这种方式产生了"……被爱慕和为他人活着的需求"。[7]

德·波伏娃认为，只有存在主义思想才能真正阐明这些观点，因为它允许女人不以其所处的社会环境强加给她们的那些观念来想象自己。存在主义"自由意志"的基本观点——人能够塑造自己的生活轨迹——为女人从社会的约束中和重压下解放自己提供了一条途径："所有个体的人生之路……都有一个存在主义的基础，该基础让我们从整体上理解人存在的特殊形式，即我们所谓的人生。"[8]

女性受压制的境况源自社会对女人的看法，即不把女人看作个体，而是看作一个存在物，"这个存在物被要求使自己成为客体。"[9]不过，这一切都是可以改变的。既然女性气质是后天习得的，那么，它也可以被主动放弃。性别不平等并非建立在男女身体的差异之上，而是建立在对这些差异的解释之上。对这种解释进行质疑的女性能够掌控自己的生活。德·波伏娃的存在主义方法为理解女性

24

受压制的根源以及克服这一境况提供了路径。

时代贡献

《第二性》最具原创性和持续性的成就之一就是它质疑了由来已久的有关女人的文化神话，并且证明它们已经渗透到从文学、艺术到心理学等文化领域的各个方面。德·波伏娃提醒说，学者受这些神话的影响在所难免，毕竟它们也是更为广义的文化的一部分。

德·波伏娃特别指出了诸如"邪恶的后妈"（她诱奸鳏夫并奴役他的孩子）和"性感十足的女人"（她不会与男人踏实过日子）这样的流行神话。这些神话不断出现在西方文化中，包括在医疗评估和精神病学档案中。她指出，医生都没有可用于描述"女色情狂"（该词用以描述性欲过度旺盛的女人）的男性版本的术语。"女色情狂"这样的术语强化了这样一种观念，即女人拥有如此强烈的性欲实属不正常。

德·波伏娃最具原创性和最为重要的见解是，人们对女人的各种期望是互不相容的：女人不能同时成为性感的勾引者、贞洁的圣女、自我牺牲的母亲、孩子般的无邪少女 * 以及羞怯的家庭主妇。要想完成这一项不可能完成的任务，就意味着女人无法培养自己独立或一致的身份。[10]

---

1. 西蒙娜·德·波伏娃：《第二性》，H. M. 帕什利译，纽约：艾尔弗雷德·A. 克诺夫出版社，1953 年，第 172 页。

2. 德·波伏娃：《第二性》，第 381 页。

3. 德·波伏娃：《第二性》，第 382 页。

4. 德·波伏娃：《第二性》，第 119 页。

5. 德·波伏娃：《第二性》，第 304 页。

6. 德·波伏娃：《第二性》，第 304 页。

7. 德·波伏娃：《第二性》，第 304 页。

8. 德·波伏娃：《第二性》，第 54 页。

9. 德·波伏娃：《第二性》，第 381 页。

10. 德·波伏娃：《第二性》，第 185 页。

第二部分：学术思想

5 思想主脉

要点 ⚷

- 西蒙娜·德·波伏娃在《第二性》中提出，世界总是围绕着男人的利益运转。

- 德·波伏娃坚定地认为，如果文明要进步的话，必须像对待男人那样平等地对待女人。

- 她追溯了妇女处于次要地位的悠久历史，认为她们实际上被当作客体来对待。她还审视了流行观念背后女性的实际境况。

核心主题

在《第二性》中，西蒙娜·德·波伏娃回顾了人类悠久的历史，勾勒出从古至今女人受压迫的境况。她认为，世界首先是为了男人的利益而运转，其次才是为了女人的利益。

她对这个父权社会的质疑涵盖了以下几个主题：性别平等、女性的物化＊（把女人当作客体来对待）、社会经济的不公平以及文化神话如何影响人们的举止和思维方式。

德·波伏娃首先分析了生活中每个领域的性别关系＊，包括家庭与工作场所、社会领域与政治、文学与艺术、宗教与大众文化。她讨论了女人的二等公民地位的根源，并探讨了女人受压迫对整个社会意味着什么。

该书对与女性气质有关的根深蒂固的观念进行研究，展示了女人如何从童年起就受到教导，从而认为自己不如男人。德·波伏娃有关性别关系的分析揭示了女人的一生如何被她们充满野心和欲望的父亲、兄弟与丈夫塑造："塑造女人就是塑造一个绝对的他者，不存在对等关系，罔顾一切经验，否认她是一个主体、一个人。"[1] 德·波伏娃指出，像婚姻这样的传统制度用妻子、母亲、仆人和保姆这些角色来约束女人，从而导致她们受到奴役。

德·波伏娃的主要观点是，这些压迫性力量不仅对女人造成伤害，而且会殃及整个社会。她提出，两性平等对于人类的进步是必要的，而且女性的解放将使整个社会受益。在《第二性》中，她拥护平等主义*，该主义认为所有人都应该得到平等的对待。她坚持认为，虽然男女在本质上并无差异，但是社会却对他们区别对待。

> "承认女人是人并不是要剥夺男人的经验……抛弃神话也不是要破坏两性间的所有戏剧性关系……这并不是要废除诗歌、爱情、冒险、幸福、梦想，而只是要求行为、情感和激情建立在事实的基础之上。"
>
> —— 西蒙娜·德·波伏娃：《第二性》

思想探究

《第二性》认为，人类有史以来妇女便遭受压迫。这使得妇女解放（或自由）的斗争难上加难，其原因在于女性不像犹太人或者非裔美国人那样，她们没有过得到自由的经历，也没有共同的历史。[2]

德·波伏娃提出，妇女从未同时在家庭和公共空间拥有影响力。例如，她注意到古希腊女性具有一些合法权力，比如她们有权买卖财产，但是实际上她们在家里几乎没有权力；妇女的活动场所仅限于住宅后部，母亲甚至无权过问子女的教育问题。[3] 在古罗马，妇女的状况则相反，她们没有合法权力，但是占据着住宅的中心地位，并且对仆人和子女的家庭教师有一定的处置权。在德·波伏娃看来，这些例子证明，女人以牺牲家庭自由为代价获得合法自由，以牺牲合法自由为代价获得家庭自由，只有男人才同时拥有这两者。

这就意味着"女人的社会地位是由男人分配的，她从来没有施行过自己的法律。"因为男人有更大的经济、政治和社会权力，所以他们在文化和历史事件中也扮演着更为重要的角色。德·波伏娃注意到，"不是因为女人地位低下，所以她们在历史上无关紧要，而是因为她们在历史上无关紧要，所以她们的地位注定低下。"[4]

德·波伏娃指出，女人这种低下的地位影响其经历的所有方面。基于"身份是后天产生的，而非生来就有的"这一存在主义的观点，德·波伏娃认为，"一个女人不是天生的，而是后天造就的。"[5]换句话说，女性气质是后天习得的。这个定义女性气质的标准必定会导致女人认为自己低人一等。

对于德·波伏娃而言，女性气质是一种潜含政治意味的社会建构。这就意味着我们对女性气质行为的理解受到习俗、文化和语言的影响，而这些因素都旨在强调女性的地位低于男性。我们将女性气质与身体羸弱和情感脆弱联系在一起，这就强化了女性不适合参与工作或者担任领导职位的观念。

语言表述

德·波伏娃首先将自己视为小说家和自传作家，这可能是她的哲学著作比其同辈的著作更通俗易懂的原因。与思想家兼其伴侣让-保罗·萨特的著作相比，德·波伏娃的著作基本上不用专业术语。她假定读者对精神分析学或存在主义思想知之甚少，并且在给出反对某些观点的理由之前，阐明那些费解的理论概念。

对于英文读者而言，阅读《第二性》遇到的一大困难是该书遭到了不少删节。该书的法语原版有 900 多页，但是它的第一位译者 H. M. 帕什利*删掉了将近 300 页的内容。他删掉了两个最重要的部分，包括有关历史的讨论和有关婚姻的论文。

哲学家玛格丽特·西蒙斯*提出，帕什利作为一名动物学家，没有资格翻译一部哲学著作，而因为他翻译了这本书，所以它遭了殃。首先，帕什利频繁使用的语句削弱了德·波伏娃的观点。例如，他把意指"humanity"（人类）的法语词"humanité"翻译为"mankind"（人类；男性）。[6] 他还错译了许多重要的哲学概念。德·波伏娃和萨特用来指代"人的意识"的存在主义术语是"etre-pour-soi"，其标准的英文翻译应该是"being-for-itself"（自身的存在）——暗含"潜在的自由意识"之意。但是帕什利把它翻译成各种版本的"根据人的真实本性"，歪曲了它的意思。

虽然这些问题并不一定会降低该书对主流读者的影响（毕竟对他们来说，存在主义是很陌生的），但是帕什利的英文译本确实影响了学界对该书的批评反应以及说英语的哲学家对该书的使用。[7]

几十年来，德·波伏娃的英语出版商艾尔弗雷德·A. 克诺夫都没有理睬法国学者想要重译该书并补充漏译部分的请求。直到 2009 年，新版的《第二性》英文版才得以面世。2012 年，《第二性》再版，补充了第一版中缺失的内容——包括帕什利删掉的历史上许多妇女的传记。但是，研究德·波伏娃的学者托里·莫伊*声称这些新的版本也有许多误译，并对此提出了尖锐的批评。[8] 而重要的是，任何研读该书译本的读者至少要意识到这些问题。

1. 西蒙娜·德·波伏娃:《第二性》,H. M. 帕什利译,纽约:艾尔弗雷德·A.克诺夫出版社,1953 年,第 238 页。

2. 德·波伏娃:《第二性》,第 xviii 页。

3. 德·波伏娃:《第二性》,第 124 页。

4. 德·波伏娃:《第二性》,第 71 页。

5. 德·波伏娃:《第二性》,第 122 页。

6. 玛格丽特·A.西蒙斯:"西蒙娜·德·波伏娃的沉默:猜猜《第二性》缺失了什么",《妇女研究国际论坛》第 6 卷,1983 年第 5 期,第 559—664 页。也可参阅玛格丽特·A.西蒙斯:"《第二性》:从马克思主义到激进女权主义",《女性主义解读西蒙娜·德·波伏娃》,玛格丽特·A.西蒙斯编,宾夕法尼亚州立大学帕克分校:宾夕法尼亚州立大学出版社,1995 年,第 243—262 页。

7. 西蒙斯:"《第二性》"。

8. 托里·莫伊:"淫妇",《伦敦书评》第 32 卷,2010 年 2 月第 11 期,登录日期 2015 年 2 月 2 日,https://www.lrb.co.uk/v32/n03/torilmoi/the-adulteress-wife。

6 思想支脉

要点 🔑

- 《第二性》审视了所有文化领域中的女性形象，尤其是那些体现"母亲身份和性行为相互排斥"这一观念的形象。

- 德·波伏娃认为，人们通常认为，不遵从社会规则的女人"野气十足"，需要被驯服。

- 她认为剥夺女人的贞操就是男人维护自己权力的需要。这一思路可以追溯到与当今女性割礼*有关的问题。

其他思想

西蒙娜·德·波伏娃的《第二性》深入研究了相关的文化神话，这些神话有助于加强我们对女性性行为的理解，其中首先是关于母亲和妓女的神话。德·波伏娃将这一神话的力量归因于社会对母亲身份的尊敬以及"母亲身份和性行为相互排斥"这种看法。

纵观人类的整个历史和各种文化，女人的主要目的就是嫁人，并为丈夫传宗接代。[1] 母亲之所以受到尊重，是因为她通过繁衍后代来帮助族群延续下去，而那些拒绝母亲身份的女人会受到污蔑或被赋予消极的形象。女人的滥交和不忠破坏了婚姻制度和母亲身份，[2] 所以这样的女人被贴上了淫妇的标签。[3] "未婚母亲会引起丑闻，而对于孩子来说，他的出生则是一个污点"，[4] 而不忠的妻子则会被活活烧死或被石头砸死。

德·波伏娃指出，社会并未用相同的标准去要求男人。"出于谨慎的考虑，男人要妻子发誓为他守节，但他自己却不满足于这种强迫女人遵守的守节要求。"[5] 这是因为社会认为"婚姻会扼杀爱情"，而丈夫倾向于认为妻子"与其说是爱人，倒不如说是孩子的母亲"。[6] 对于失意的丈夫而言，不忠和嫖娼仅仅是性释放的有效手段。"妓女之于城市，就如下水道之于宫殿"[7] 的说法阐释了卖淫的实际作用。就像下水道能够使宫殿清洁，确保居民不会在自己的污秽中腐烂发臭一样，妓女让已婚男人定期"排解"他们的性挫折，以维持他们婚姻的完整和社会的运转。"妓女是替罪羊；男人在她身上发泄自己的卑鄙堕落。"[8]

德·波伏娃认为，母亲、淫妇和妓女三者共同运作，以维护婚姻制度。"与被神圣化的女人形成鲜明对比的是，坏女人却能得到完全的解脱。"[9] 淫妇的神话建立在母亲身份被理想化的基础之上。同样，"'不知羞耻的女人'这一社会等级"——妓女——"允许'诚实的女人'得到男人最有礼貌的尊重"。[10]

> "女人最基本的问题之一……是她的生育角色和她的生产劳动之间的协调一致。历史伊始，女人就注定要从事家务劳动，并被阻止参与对世界的塑造，这一基本事实体现了生殖功能对她的束缚。"
>
> —— 西蒙娜·德·波伏娃：《第二性》

思想探究

德·波伏娃还指出，与女性解放相关的所有特点——性格坚毅、思想独立、反对权威——都与社会想要驯服的那个野气十足的女性形象组合到了一起。[11] 但是，社会也认为，当对手或猎物反抗时，征服会更让人愉快。因此，人们允许这个固执己见的女人说出她的想法，这不是因为社会想要倾听，而是因为社会以阻止她发声为乐。"男人是一个事物的主人，而当这个事物在不断地逃避控制时，它就更值得被掌控。"[12]

德·波伏娃展示了这个神话是如何渗入文学的。在文学作品中，一个男人经常和一个胆大的女人较量，而这个女人最终会屈服于他的意志。德·波伏娃引证了威廉·莎士比亚的《驯悍记》（1590—1593）*。在剧中，男主人公彼特鲁乔使用心理学的花招赢回并驯服了有主见的凯特琳娜。最后，凯特琳娜被驯服得服服帖帖，而彼特鲁乔"叫他的邻居来看看他能够征服他的妻子是多么地有威严"。[13]

女性解放的历史性人物，比如妇女参政论者*（为妇女的投票权奋斗的女人）和女学究*（"蓝丝袜"，指女性知识分子），同样被视为有待驯服的野蛮动物。德·波伏娃注意到，一个追求解放的女人或被视为一个悍妇——一个特别有主见的女人——或被视为性诱惑的来源。无论哪一种，她都面临着自己所真正要求的东西——解放——不被听见的风险。

被忽视之处

虽然人们对德·波伏娃有关母亲身份和性欲望的观点进行了广泛的探讨，但是大多忽视了她对与童贞有关的神话的解读。这一领域亟待进一步研究，因为它与目前有关女性割礼的讨论相关。女性割礼的仪式在非洲、亚洲和中东的许多国家以及世界上其他一些地区实行，目的是要控制女人的性行为。之所以进行阴蒂切除术（外阴蒂的切除），是为了阻止女性获得性快感，而锁阴术（阴唇的缝合）则是为了使一个女人在婚前保持童贞：这标志着她成为一个封闭的空间，将由其丈夫打开。与女性割礼相关的象征意义给《第二性》及其关于处女的论述增添了新的解读视角。

德·波伏娃把夺取女人贞操的行为等同于权力。处女是男人希望自己能独占的一个欲望客体："要确保我对某物的所有权，最可靠的方法就是阻止别人使用它。"[14] 不仅如此，因为"在一个男人看来，没有什么比从未属于任何人的东西更令人向往，"所以德·波伏娃明确地把夺取女人的贞操和吞并无人占用的土地联系到了一起。[15] 这些都是一个男人通过占有的行为来"证明"自己的方式。

夺取女人的贞操可以让男人重新肯定自己。"男人通过在身体上占有一个人来满足自己的存在感。"[16] 在原始时代，婚姻是一种绑架形式："（丈夫）强行带走他的妻子，来证明他有能力获得陌生人的财富，并冲破命运的束缚。"[17] 对于德·波伏娃而言，性行为与暴力、权力联系在一起。同样，女性割礼建立在处女神话的基础上，强调妇女是交换或征服的对象，她们的身体需要受到男人的支配。

1. 西蒙娜·德·波伏娃：《第二性》，H. M. 帕什利译，纽约：艾尔弗雷德·A. 克诺夫出版社，1953 年，第 523 页。

2. 德·波伏娃：《第二性》，第 178 页。

3. 德·波伏娃：《第二性》，第 177 页。

4. 德·波伏娃：《第二性》，第 177 页。

5. 德·波伏娃：《第二性》，第 523 页。

6. 德·波伏娃：《第二性》，第 524 页。

7. 德·波伏娃：《第二性》，第 95 页。

8. 德·波伏娃：《第二性》，第 524 页。

9. 德·波伏娃：《第二性》，第 179 页。

10. 德·波伏娃：《第二性》，第 524 页。

11. 德·波伏娃：《第二性》，第 143 页。

12. 德·波伏娃：《第二性》，第 164 页。

13. 德·波伏娃：《第二性》，第 95 页。

14. 德·波伏娃：《第二性》，第 143 页。

15. 德·波伏娃：《第二性》，第 143 页。

16. 德·波伏娃：《第二性》，第 131 页。

17. 德·波伏娃：《第二性》，第 68 页。

7 历史成就

要点 ⚷

- 西蒙娜·德·波伏娃凭借《第二性》成功地促使人们关注妇女低下的社会地位，以及她们在学术界、文学界、艺术界和政治领域处于几近缺失状态的原因。
- 该书因其激进的观点而极具开创性，以至于被罗马天主教会 * 列入禁书名单。
- 我们可以认为该书已经过时，但这只能说明波伏娃的观点多么成功地改变了社会。

观点评价

西蒙娜·德·波伏娃的《第二性》对社会如何迫使妇女处于从属地位这一问题进行了前所未有的抨击。该书阐明了性别歧视如何贯穿人类的历史，并提请人们注意女性在哲学、心理学和历史等学术领域的缺失状态。

波伏娃的许多论点令人耳目一新，对战后法国保守的价值观予以挑战。当谈到女大学毕业生数量稀少的问题时，德·波伏娃举出了一项调查：大多数女性受访者同意"男孩比女孩强，他们是更优秀的工作者。"[1] 德·波伏娃认为，女人从小就被教导着认为自己不如男人有能力，这种观点限制了她们的雄心壮志和成功的机会。职业女性认为："她如果能够挣钱养活自己，那就足以让人赞叹，因为她本可以把命运托付给一个男人的。"[2]

围绕"在家庭之外，女人有望获得怎样的成功"这一问题，该书进行了一场激进的全新讨论。虽然在该书出版 20 年后，法国妇女才开始在工作场所崭露头角，但是它的出版是妇女摆脱传统角色走向解放的重要一步。

德·波伏娃也是第一位公开向社会对女性性行为的假设进行质疑的作家。她在有关社会生活的章节里告诉我们："据说女人不像男人那般需要性行为，其实不然。"[3] 她指出，这些观念源自这一事实："性爱仍被认为是女人提供给男人的一项服务，因此它也使男人看起来好像是她的主人。"[4] 她在书中的其他地方写道，堕胎和避孕是一项权利，女人有权享受性快感，而且应该享有是否生育和何时生育的自由选择权。[5] 这些言论对法国有关婚姻和性关系的根深蒂固的观念提出了挑战，并且预示了十多年后才发生的性革命*。

> "不是因为（女人）地位低下，所以她们在历史上无关紧要，而是因为她们在历史上无关紧要，所以她们的地位注定低下。"
>
> —— 西蒙娜·德·波伏娃：《第二性》

当时的成就

德·波伏娃的著作之所以成就卓著，不仅在于其论证的严谨和观点的巨大影响力，还在于其大胆无畏的特点。该书毫不隐讳的内容和激进的观点与当时强烈的保守主义和提高出生率主义（即对生育的拥护）南辕北辙。

第二次世界大战期间，从 1940 年至 1944 年统治法国的维希政权*只是勉强允许妇女出去工作，而且将分发避孕药具列为应受惩罚的罪行。[6] 家庭主妇玛丽-珍妮·拉图尔因堕胎在 1943 年被送上了断头台。[7] 尽管妇女因在抵制纳粹 * 占领的法国抵抗军 * 中发挥重要作用而获得投票权，但是罗马天主教会和政府都依旧强调母亲身份和家庭的重要性。而一个女人，比如德·波伏娃，讨论女性的性行为并公开质疑生育的可取程度，这样的做法是令人震惊的。

德·波伏娃审视性别关系的方式和她对女性性高潮的明确描述（并非依据正常的生理状况，而是在"受试者的整个生活状况"[8] 下进行的）被人们视为对性道德的冒犯。她认为，激进的性学家阿尔弗雷德·金赛对女性自慰人数的估算是有限的，而实际数量远比他所宣称的要"多得多"[9]，这体现了她的观点在当时是多么的极端。

该书大胆直白的内容导致梵蒂冈教会将其列入禁书的索引 * 之中，直至今日。[10] 德·波伏娃还收到了男读者义愤填膺的来信，他们对她的侮辱性称呼五花八门，从"性欲未得到满足"和"性冷淡"到"女色情狂"和"女同性恋"。[11] 与此同时，该书显然也对主流社会产生了影响。据该书出版几十年之后的一些采访披露，有许多法国女人偷偷阅读了此书，并且深受其观点的启发。[12] 在以英语为母语的国家中，人们对《第二性》的反应没有那么强烈，其中部分原因是罗马天主教会的地位不是那么突出，另一部分原因是英美读者不像法国读者那样认为该书是对其文化的恶意攻击。[13]

局限性

《第二性》是时代的产物。它的出版先于许多重大事件，如口服避孕药的发明、堕胎在法国的合法化、性革命和同性恋权利运动 *。在德·波伏娃撰写该书时，女性在法国的劳动力中占少数，而且当时很少有女大学毕业生。自那时起，女性在社会中的角色已经发生了根本变化，今天很少有读者会像 1949 年的第一批读者那样对该书的内容感到震惊。

然而，德·波伏娃的著作已经过时这一事实正是该书获得成功的明显标志。《第二性》之所以能够载入史册，正是因为它挑战并继而改变了西方社会。得益于德·波伏娃的努力，西方妇女如今生活在一个与她的描述截然不同的世界中。

《第二性》也遭到了一些法国女权主义者的批评，她们认为该书对女性怀有敌意。德·波伏娃拥护平等主义，意在消除社会建构的 * 人与人之间的差异。对她而言，女性气质是一种建构，其实男人和女人并没有什么差异，人的生理不代表人的命运。20 世纪 60 年代以来，法国女权主义第二次浪潮 * 中的女权主义者，如露丝·伊利格瑞 *、埃莱娜·西苏 *、安托瓦内特·富克 * 和朱莉娅·克里斯蒂娃 *，认为德·波伏娃无视性别差异的努力是在迫使女人吸收父权制的价值观，变成男人。

随着这一代法国女权主义者将传统的女性活动作为有效的经验形式加以重新利用，她们与德·波伏娃逐渐拉开了距离。今天，德·波伏娃的著作在她的祖国比在美国和英国应用得更少。[14] 当她在 1986 年去世以后，福柯建议说，既然德·波伏娃已经下葬，法国的女权主义者可以忘记她的"普世主义的、平等主义的、同化的和正常化的女权主义立场"，并迈进 21 世纪。[15]

---

1. 西蒙娜·德·波伏娃：《第二性》，H. M. 帕什利译，纽约：艾尔弗雷德·A. 克诺夫出版社，1953 年，第 658 页。

2. 德·波伏娃：《第二性》，第 658 页。

3. 德·波伏娃：《第二性》，第 521 页。

4. 德·波伏娃：《第二性》，第 521 页。

5. 德·波伏娃：《第二性》，第 464 页。

6. 托里·莫伊：《西蒙娜·德·波伏娃：一位知识女性的塑造》，纽约：牛津大学出版社，1994 年，第 187 页。也可参阅弗朗辛·穆尔－德雷福斯：《维希和永恒的女性》，巴黎：修伊尔出版社，1996 年。

7. 希拉·罗博特姆："前言"，《第二性》，西蒙娜·德·波伏娃著，坎迪斯·博德和希拉·马洛瓦尼－谢瓦里埃译，纽约：佳酿出版社，2009 年。

8. 德·波伏娃：《第二性》，第 71 页。

9. 德·波伏娃：《第二性》，第 71 页。

10. 伊丽莎白·拉德森："审查制度"，《全球史》，迈克·F. 苏亚雷斯和 H.R. 沃乌德惠森编，牛津：牛津大学出版社，2013 年，第 173 页。

11. 索尼亚·克鲁克斯：《西蒙娜·德·波伏娃与模糊政治学》，牛津：牛津大学出版社，2012 年，第 48 页。

12. 凯瑟琳·罗杰斯："《第二性》对法国女权主义场景的影响"，《西蒙娜·德·波伏娃的〈第二性〉：新跨学科杂文》，露丝·埃文斯编，曼彻斯特：曼彻斯特大学出版社，1998 年，第 67 页。

13. 玛格丽特·A. 西蒙斯："西蒙娜·德·波伏娃的沉默"，《女性研究国际论坛》第 6 卷，1983 年第 5 期，第 559—664 页。

14. 莫伊：《西蒙娜·德·波伏娃》，第 97—98 页。

15. 莫伊：《西蒙娜·德·波伏娃》，第 97 页。

8 著作地位

要点 🔑

- 德·波伏娃后来认为，她在《第二性》中表达的观点虽然在 1949 年显得十分激进，但事实上激进的程度还不够。

- 德·波伏娃表示，她的伴侣让-保罗·萨特首先敦劝她审视妇女的社会境况。此后，学者们一直质疑这一说法。

- 尽管德·波伏娃出版了许多小说和回忆录，但《第二性》仍然是她最著名和最受好评的著作。

定位

西蒙娜·德·波伏娃在 1946 年开始撰写《第二性》，此时距离其第一部小说《女宾》的发表已有三年。她在 14 个月内完成了这本著作，同时撰写了另一篇题为《模糊伦理学》的文章，并将《第二性》的摘录发表在《摩登时代》*上。该杂志是她和她的伴侣兼思想家让-保罗·萨特在 1945 年创办的。

《第二性》是德·波伏娃职业生涯早期的成果，在她致力于女权主义运动之前就已经写就。直到很久以后，当她在 1972 年加入妇女解放运动*时，德·波伏娃才宣布自己是女权主义者。[1] 同年，在接受女权主义出版商爱丽丝·施瓦泽尔题为"革命的女人"的采访时，德·波伏娃称《第二性》的激进程度还不够。她曾相信社会主义可以解放妇女，因此没有必要进行女权主义斗争。但是，当她看到社会主义和资本主义一样无法改善女性处境时，她改变了她的看法。[2]

1976 年，在接受约翰·杰拉西的采访时，德·波伏娃也承认，

《第二性》的理论性太强，并且因只关注白人中产阶级女性的状况和她的个人经历而具有局限性。她相信，女权主义现在需要的是一本"植根于实践"的书，并且能够由"来自各个国家各个阶层的全体妇女"来撰写。[3]

德·波伏娃还修正了她早期的观点，即女人对其丈夫的忠诚使得她们之间很难实现团结。在目睹了20世纪60年代工厂女工的罢工之后，德·波伏娃改变了这一观点。当她们的丈夫抱怨时，这些工人阶级妇女就聚集起来反抗："她们开始致力于一种双重的斗争：一方面是反抗（工厂）老板、警察、政府等的阶级斗争，另一方面是反抗其丈夫的性别斗争。"[4]

> "我只是展现了我们的社会中女性所遭遇的现实。我的读者有责任从她们的遭遇和经历中吸取教训，并使自己免受同样的遭遇。"
>
> —— 西蒙娜·德·波伏娃，
> 引自迪尔德丽·贝尔：《西蒙娜·德·波伏娃：传记》

整合

在她1963年出版的自传《环境的力量》中，德·波伏娃实际上回忆了一个心灵得到启示的时刻。当时，她明白了"这是一个男性的世界"，而她的童年是"由男人创造的神话所支撑的"。[5]她表示，正是她的伴侣兼存在主义作家让-保罗·萨特督促她审视女性的社会境况的。

最近，玛格丽特·西蒙斯、爱德华和凯特·富布鲁克*等学者都质疑了这一说法的真实性。在德·波伏娃去世后出版的日记表明，早在她在巴黎高等师范学院攻读哲学的研究生时代，她就已经运用存在主义思想分析妇女的境况了。[6] 因此，《第二性》既可被视为德·波伏娃女权主义思想的开端，也可被视为她公开表达自己观点的第一次尝试。

无论如何，该书因其对存在主义思想的重要贡献以及它将哲学分析与自传性反思相结合的写作手法而脱颖而出，这始终是德·波伏娃著作的一个典型特征。她从未声称自己没有偏见，而是通过自己作为女性的经历，以自己的愤怒为《第二性》增添了力量。[7]

就像《女宾》（1943）和后来的《名士风流》（1954）一样，《第二性》面向的是了解德·波伏娃有关性行为的非正统观点以及她与萨特的开放式关系的读者。她的这一激进形象，既积极又消极地影响了读者对《第二性》的反应。这引起了激烈的争议，但也使她成为一名女英雄，成为性自由的象征。[8] 对于她的支持者来说，她与萨特开放的、无子女的关系证明了女性可以追求除婚姻或母亲身份之外的东西。

意义

《第二性》是德·波伏娃最著名的著作。虽然她的小说和早期的散文局限于文学批评和哲学领域，但是《第二性》却影响了包括社会学、历史和政治学 * 在内的多种学科的学术研究。它还影响了女权主义历史研究和酷儿理论等分支学科的研究。

在政治学领域，吉尔·安德伍德和胡尔希德·瓦迪亚就德·波伏娃的一些观点和行动发表了评论。德·波伏娃认为，法国的女权主义与制度主义政治学的关系不太和谐；她作为妇女解放运动的成员，努力在不依靠政党政治的情况下使堕胎合法化。[9] 对于这些学者来说，《第二性》为他们思考法国女权主义运动的反议会主义——即反对并试图推翻政治体制——的历史提供了一个重要的起点。

对于英美女权主义批评家而言，《第二性》始终是一份重要的文献。他们在演讲厅和更广阔的世界把该书的观点应用于对妇女权利的讨论中。像卡米尔·帕利亚*和朱迪斯·巴特勒*这样有影响力的美国女权主义者都认为波伏娃对她们的著作产生了重要影响。[10]德·波伏娃的观点散见于许多介绍女权主义思想的著作中，尤其是那些与"被塑造成"一个女人和生殖对性别压迫所起的作用相关的著作。

德·波伏娃在分析中认为妇女的生殖角色是由社会建构的，女权主义学者弗雷德里卡·斯卡思利用这一分析来思考"在早期游牧社会环境中，妇女在生物层面上所经历的物种奴役是如何在父权制下被非法重现的"。[11]这意味着妇女作为母亲的生物角色被用来将她们限制在像家庭这样的特定场所之内，以及被用来否认她们的其他身份。斯卡思利用波伏娃的观点来讨论母亲身份的政治性特征。最近，在《哲学中的女人：需要改变什么？》（2013）中，卡琳娜·哈奇森和菲奥纳·詹金斯*认为，《第二性》是第一本试图质问妇女为何被排除在哲学辩论之外的著作。她们指出，目前情况并没有改变：在学科中"排斥女人，或者说，培养男人"仍然是一个迫切的问题。[12]德·波伏娃的著作对这些当代争论仍有参考价值。

---

1. 克莱尔·洛比耶：《法国妇女的状况：从 1945 至今——纪录片选集》，伦敦：劳特利奇出版社，1992 年，第 19 页。

2. 爱丽丝·施瓦泽尔：《第二性之后：与西蒙娜·德·波伏娃的对话》，伦敦：名士出版社，1984 年。

3. 约翰·杰拉西："西蒙娜·德·波伏娃访谈录：《第二性》25 年后"，《社会》，1976 年 1—2 月，登录日期 2015 年 5 月 5 日，http://www.marxists.org/reference/subject/ethics/de-beauvoir/1976/interview.htm。

4. 杰拉西："西蒙娜·德·波伏娃访谈录"。

5. 琼·雷顿：《西蒙娜·德·波伏娃与妇女》，新泽西州麦迪逊：菲尔莱迪金森大学，1975 年，第 24 页。

6. 南希·鲍尔："我们必须阅读德·波伏娃吗？"，《西蒙娜·德·波伏娃的遗产》，埃米莉·格罗肖兹编，纽约：牛津大学出版社，2004 年，第 125 页。

7. 德·波伏娃："对话"。

8. 《德·波伏娃的女儿》，彭妮·福斯特制作的电影，1988 年。

9. 吉尔·安德伍德和胡尔希德·瓦迪亚：《法国的妇女与政治：1958—2000》，伦敦和纽约：劳特利奇出版社，2000 年，第 156 页。

10. 卡米尔·帕利亚：《性、艺术与美国文化散文集》，纽约：企鹅出版社；朱迪斯·巴特勒：《性别麻烦——女权主义与身份的颠覆》，伦敦：劳特利奇出版社，1990 年。

11. 弗雷德里卡·斯卡思：《另一个内在：西蒙娜·德·波伏娃的伦理、政治与身体》，纽约：罗曼和利特菲尔德出版社，2004 年，第 141—142 页。

12. 卡琳娜·哈奇森和菲奥纳·詹金斯：《哲学中的女人：需要改变什么？》，牛津：牛津大学出版社，2013 年，第 9 页。

第三部分：学术影响

9 最初反响

要点 🔑

- 当《第二性》在 1949 年问世时，许多评论家抨击该书是对当时性道德极端无礼的侮辱。

- 德·波伏娃在法国遭到公开嘲笑和侮辱，但是以英语为母语的读者更倾向于接受她的观点。

- 《第二性》对德·波伏娃之后的法国女权主义者究竟有多大影响？关于这一问题有很多激烈的争论。

批评

第二次世界大战之后，法国社会非常保守。西蒙娜·德·波伏娃在《第二性》中对社会礼仪和性规范的直接挑战激起了人们的暴怒，以至于罗马天主教小说家弗朗索瓦·莫里亚克*以该书为基础开展了一场反对"文学中的堕落"的运动。[1]某份保守报纸上的一篇文章称该书是"为性倒错和堕胎所做的令人作呕的道歉"。[2]

法国政治左派认为该书是资产阶级（中产阶级）的堕落之作，因而对其不屑一顾。人们批评它"宣扬人性中最低劣的特点：兽性本能和性堕落"。[3]左翼哲学家阿尔贝·加缪*说，该书使法国男人显得荒唐可笑。[4]然而，根据德·波伏娃的朋友、人类学家克劳德·列维-施特劳斯*的说法，这是因为"（当权者）难以忍受一位女存在主义者"。[5]

法国始终普遍存在着对该书的负面看法，而评论家的理由是，德·波伏娃在为让−保罗·萨特诱惑年轻女性时所扮演的角色破坏了她的女权主义原则。[6] 他们谴责她未能认识到其恋人、哲学家萨特对自己和其他女人缺乏尊重，因为在引诱这些女人并将她们引荐给萨特的过程中，她使自己成为萨特偷欢的工具和剥削这些女人的帮手。德·波伏娃在 1939 年诱惑的那个学生当时还未成年，因此，她还被指责剥削更为年轻的女人。另外，她还被指责试图废除与允许进行性行为的年龄相关的法律。[7] 让−雷蒙德·奥代特将《第二性》描述为一部极度"自恋"*的作品。[8] 除了引人注目的女权主义哲学家米歇尔·勒德夫*之外，当今法国对《第二性》感兴趣的知识分子很少。在《希帕奇亚的选择》（1990）中，德夫从德·波伏娃与哲学之间困难重重的关系以及萨特对妇女明显的蔑视态度这些方面来审视《第二性》。[9]

英国和美国对《第二性》的接受度更高。1980 年至 1992 年间出版了 20 本关于德·波伏娃的书，其中有 17 本是用英文写的。[10] 伊莱恩·马克斯*在 1973 年出版的《西蒙娜·德·波伏娃：与死亡相遇》是第一部研究德·波伏娃作品的英语著作，该书也向更为广泛的读者群介绍了《第二性》。

这些学者认为，法国人对德·波伏娃的批评常常体现出一种对妇女毫不隐晦的厌恶之情。挪威裔美国女权主义作家托里·莫伊指出："这意味着无论一个女人说什么、写什么或者想什么，都不比她的身份是什么更重要。"[11] 因此，把德·波伏娃描绘成自恋狂或者萨特的奴隶能有效地使她非政治化，从而将《第二性》贬低为一个过于情绪化的女人的咆哮。[12]

> "实际上，两性关系并不完全像电的正负两极的关系一样：男人代表积极和中性这两面，正如'男人'一词常被用来指代人类；而女人只代表消极的一面，并且受到限制性标准的界定，与男人没有对等关系。"
>
> —— 西蒙娜·德·波伏娃：《第二性》

回应

《第二性》出版后不久，德·波伏娃便停止外出，以免在街上受到愤怒的读者的骚扰。[13] 她对此并不感到十分意外。她早期的一部短篇小说集，因其露骨的色情内容而被拒绝出版。德·波伏娃也经历过人们对她1943年出版的第一部小说《女宾》的强烈抗议，该小说是根据她和萨特以及她的两名女学生的绯闻改编而成的。[14]

然而，人们对《第二性》的愤慨反而使该书出名，为德·波伏娃赢得了美国出版商的关注以及多年来在国内外公开演讲的机会。其中最值得关注的是她在1975年接受的"为什么我是一个女权主义者"的电视采访，她在采访中重新提及自己写作的中心主题："成为女人并不是自然而然的事实，而是特定历史的结果。并没有生理的或心理的命运规定女人必须是这个样子的……女婴是被塑造成女人的。"[15]

《第二性》首次出版于1949年。1972年，她公开放弃了"社会主义革命会带来性别平等"的信念，并宣称自己是女权主义者。这一修正后的观点影响了她晚年的社会活动。她说，对《第二性》的任何后续修订都需要多位作者和一种实用方法。女权主义"必须从实践中得出（它的）理论，而不是相反"，并且必须反映所有阶级和文化的需求。[16] 不过，德·波伏娃从未放弃过平等主义，并且对差异化女权主义*（认为男女平等，但又有所不同）持怀疑态度。对德·波伏娃来说，"它又落入了男性的陷阱中，这个陷阱想用我们的差异把我们困住。"[17]

冲突与共识

人们围绕德·波伏娃的观点是否重要展开激烈的争论，但是《第二性》对主流读者有着明显的影响。20 世纪 70 年代以前，成千上万的法国女性在偷偷读过这本书后都深受影响。[18] 与此同时，随着 60 年代的激进运动和民众骚乱的发生，公众对《第二性》的看法也发生了转变。法国工厂的工人要求更好的工作条件，少数族裔与由来已久的种族主义*作斗争，在 1968 年还兴起了女权运动。

这是争论的起点。托里·莫伊撰写了大量关于法国女权主义无视《第二性》的论著。按照她的解读，这源于对存在主义思想的拒斥，这一思想将波伏娃变为一只"理论上的恐龙"。[19] 然而，凯瑟琳·罗杰斯*说，莫伊并不承认德·波伏娃对法国平等主义女权主义者的影响，甚至连德·波伏娃也未认识到自己的影响力。[20] 罗杰斯认为，妇女解放运动的领导人肯定读过《第二性》。她认为该书之所以未出现在那个时代的女权主义著作之中，是因为其论点早已变得平常。[21]

德·波伏娃声称，法国女权主义第二次浪潮（20 世纪 60 年代至 80 年代末）的女性参与者"可能已经成为女权主义者，其原因我在《第二性》中解释过，但是她们是在自己的生活经历中，而不是在我的书中发现了那些原因。"[22] 后来的学者继续争论她的观点是否正确。

1. 厄休拉·蒂德：《西蒙娜·德·波伏娃》，伦敦：劳特利奇出版社，2004 年，第 101 页。

2. 引自塞尔维·沙普龙：《德·波伏娃的岁月：1945—1970》，巴黎：菲亚出版社，2000 年，第 182 页；玛格丽特·A.西蒙斯："引言"，《西蒙娜·德·波伏娃：女权主义作品》，玛格丽特·A.西蒙斯和玛丽思·蒂姆曼编，芝加哥：伊利诺伊大学出版社，2015 年，第 4—5 页。

3. 引自沙普龙：《德·波伏娃的岁月》，第 175—177 页。

4. 蒂德：《西蒙娜·德·波伏娃》，第 101 页。

5. 西蒙娜·德·波伏娃：《致萨特的信》，西尔维·勒邦编，巴黎：加利玛出版社，1990 年，第 2 卷，第 284 页，引自玛格丽特·A.西蒙斯："《第二性》：从马克思主义到激进的女权主义"，《女性主义解读西蒙娜·德·波伏娃》，玛格丽特·A.西蒙斯编，宾夕法尼亚州立大学帕克分校：宾夕法尼亚州立大学出版社，1995 年，第 2 页。

6. 托里·莫伊：《西蒙娜·德·波伏娃：一位知识女性的塑造》，纽约：牛津大学出版社，1994 年，第 98 页。

7. 埃里克·伯科威茨：《性与罚：四千年的性审判史》，加利福尼亚州伯克利：对位出版社，2012 年。

8. 让-雷蒙德·奥代特：《西蒙娜·德·波伏娃：面对死亡》，洛桑：荷马时代出版社，1979 年，第 122—125 页。

9. 米歇尔·勒德夫：《希帕奇亚的选择》，特里斯坦·塞卢斯译，纽约：哥伦比亚大学出版社，1990 年。

10. 莫伊：《西蒙娜·德·波伏娃》，第 96 页。

11. 莫伊：《西蒙娜·德·波伏娃》，第 98 页。

12. 莫伊：《西蒙娜·德·波伏娃》，第 101 页。

13. 蒂德：《西蒙娜·德·波伏娃》，第 102 页。

14. 蒂德：《西蒙娜·德·波伏娃》，第 102 页。

15. 让-路易斯·瑟凡-施赖伯："为什么我是一个女权主义者：西蒙娜·德·波伏娃访谈（1975）"，登录日期 2015 年 3 月 5 日，http://www.youtube.com/watch?v=v2LkME3MMNK。

16. 约翰·杰拉西："西蒙娜·德·波伏娃访谈录：《第二性》25 年后"，《社会》，1976 年 1—2 月，登录日期 2015 年 5 月 5 日，http://www.marxists.org/reference/

subject/ethics/de-beauvoir/1976/interview.htm。

17. 玛格丽特·A.西蒙斯和杰西卡·本杰明："波伏娃访谈（1979）"，《波伏娃与〈第二性〉》，玛格丽特·A.西蒙斯编，纽约：罗曼和利特菲尔德出版社，第19页。

18. 凯瑟琳·罗杰斯："《第二性》对法国女权主义场景的影响"，《西蒙娜·德·波伏娃的〈第二性〉：新跨学科杂文》，鲁思·埃文斯编，曼彻斯特：曼彻斯特大学出版社，1998年，第64页。

19. 莫伊：《西蒙娜·德·波伏娃》，第98页。

20. 罗杰斯："《第二性》的影响"，第67页。

21. 罗杰斯："《第二性》的影响"，第64页。

22. 杰拉西："西蒙娜·德·波伏娃访谈录"。

10 后续争议

要点 🔑

- 对于德·波伏娃在定义性别时所指的含义,人们有许多不同的观点。
- 德·波伏娃的著作有助于为妇女研究*和性别研究创造学术空间。
- 人们今天阅读《第二性》是为了深入了解许多不同的事情,从性别和身份到社会经济制度怎样影响压迫等。

应用与问题

西蒙娜·德·波伏娃的《第二性》仍然存在争议,这并不完全是因为它开辟了全新的研究领域。伊丽莎白·斯佩尔曼认为,德·波伏娃因关注白人中产阶级妇女所遭受的压迫而削弱了其著作的影响力。[1]与之相反,朱迪思·奥凯利*认为这不是问题。奥凯利说,因为德·波伏娃的著作使人能够洞悉法国一整代妇女的生活,所以她有限的关注视角给人们提供了一个将德·波伏娃作为个案来研究的机会。

德·波伏娃将性别定义为一种社会建构,学者们对于该定义的效用和准确度也存在分歧。社会学、心理学和性别研究都接受了她的"不能把身份简单地归结为我们与生俱来的身体"的主张。然而,学者们倾向于认为,《第二性》明确否认性别之间存在任何实质性差异。

黛布拉·伯格芬*和莫伊拉·盖腾斯对这种方法提出了质疑。[2]两人都认为,波伏娃对"女性气质的"、"女人"和"女性的"这些概念之间关系的理解比她对性与性别之间关系的理解更为复杂。这表明波伏娃比评论家所理解的更为激进。[3] 这种新的解读方式为《第二性》作为当代性别研究的一部分提供了新的启发。

> "涉及具体行动时,女性处于失语的状态……对世界的真正控制权从未掌握在女人的手中;她们未曾给技术或经济带来影响,未曾建立或毁灭过国家,也未曾发现过新的世界。虽然一些事件由她们引发,但这些女人只是事件发生的藉口,而非真正的实施者。"
>
> —— 西蒙娜·德·波伏娃:《第二性》

思想流派

《第二性》开启了公众对女性性行为的讨论,是女权主义不可或缺的一部分。正如伊丽莎白·巴丹泰*所言,德·波伏娃的"讯息……我整代人都听到了"。[4]

从 20 世纪 70 年代以来,德·波伏娃推动了美国和加拿大妇女研究中心的创建。[5] 她的观点对性别社会学也发挥了重要作用。该学科出现于 20 世纪 50 年代中期,旨在研究人们如何指认男性气质和女性气质,以及性别是由我们的躯体决定的还是被我们受到的教育强加的。20 世纪 70 年代,在性别社会学中,女权主义方法得到了进一步发展,这种方法越来越多地采用德·波伏娃的"性别是文化的产物"这一观点。性别研究在 20 世纪 90 年代应运而生,旨在解决跨文化领域(包括文学、电影和视觉艺术)的性别认知。性别理论家探究社会化*对性别的影响,而他们的工作主要得益于德·波伏娃的观点。

在传统的男性占主导地位的哲学领域,简娜·汤普森*和多萝西·E. 史密斯*利用德·波伏娃的存在主义女性主义理论引入了一种女性视角。汤普森编辑的论文集《妇女与哲学》（1976）探讨了哲学可能如何帮助妇女的解放。她研究了许多概念，包括个人主义、身份、双性同体（女性和男性特征的结合）和自由意志。这些文章探讨女人的身份在多大程度上受到父权制价值观的限制，以及这种身份是否能够独立发展（与波伏娃的说法相反）。[6]

史密斯的著作《日常世界是有问题的：一种女权主义社会学》（1987）探讨了发展女权主义社会学的困难。"女人是什么？"这个问题提醒我们，人类是从男性的角度来观察一切的。同样，"女权主义社会学是什么？"这个问题提醒我们，这个领域是由男性的兴趣和观点塑造的。[7]《日常世界是有问题的》是挑战女权主义学术研究的重要一步，警示我们女权主义可能会进一步将妇女边缘化。

当代研究

不同的人因各种原因继续对《第二性》进行解读。朱迪斯·巴特勒和莫伊拉·盖腾斯等性别理论家认为，德·波伏娃的著作是一场更为广泛的辩论的一部分，这场辩论所涉及的问题包括性别是天生的还是后天强加的，以及一个女人能否不顾自己作为"他者"的状态而塑造自己的身份。

女权主义历史学家和马克思主义思想家阅读这本书的主要目的是深入了解不同的社会经济制度（尤其是资本主义）对压迫女性所起的作用。玛丽·斯蓬伯格*在《文艺复兴以来的妇女历史书写》（2002）中指出，德·波伏娃的观点是解释"妇女没有参与历史"这一认识的关键。[8]

　　女性主义理论的导论经常提到《第二性》，把它作为女权主义思想的一个里程碑以及思考人文科学的一个重要的女性视角。安德里亚·奈*在《女权主义理论与人的哲学》（2013）中称赞道，在父权制价值观持续使哲学思想和文学阐释蒙受阴影的情况下，德·波伏娃的观点一直具有现实意义。[9]

　　哲学家们始终对作家兼哲学家让-保罗·萨特如何影响了德·波伏娃的著作持有兴趣。起初，他们认为《第二性》深受萨特观点的影响，这导致一些人质疑该书的原创性，甚至认为它自相矛盾。萨特的厌女症*是有据可查的，他的哲学也饱含厌女色彩，一个女权主义者怎么可能把她的著作建立在这样一门哲学之上呢？[10]但是伯格芬和克里斯廷·戴格尔*用德·波伏娃的日记来证明她的想法在她和萨特建立关系之前就产生了。实际上，是德·波伏娃对萨特的著作产生了影响。[11]这一争论的产物便是德·波伏娃研究的领军学者的论文集《萨特与德·波伏娃：影响的问题》（2009）。他们探讨的是关于萨特的影响的假设可能会如何影响学界对《第二性》的批评接受。[12]

---

1. 伊丽莎白·斯佩尔曼：《无关紧要的女性：女权主义思想中的排他性问题》，波士顿：灯塔出版社，1988 年，第 63—64 页。

2. 黛布拉·伯格芬："性别差别再叙"，以及莫伊拉·盖滕斯："德·波伏娃与生物学：第二次回顾"，《剑桥西蒙娜·德·波伏娃指南》，克劳迪娅·卡德编，剑桥：剑桥大学出版社，2003 年，第 248—265 页和第 266—285 页。

3. 莫伊拉·盖滕斯："德·波伏娃与生物学"，第 267 页；伯格芬："性别差别再叙"，第 250 页。

4. 凯瑟琳·罗杰斯："《第二性》对法国女权主义场景的影响"，《西蒙娜·德·波伏娃的〈第二性〉：新跨学科杂文》，鲁思·埃文斯编，曼彻斯特：曼彻斯特大学出版社，1998 年，第 67 页。

5. 丽莎·阿皮尼亚内西：《西蒙娜·德·波伏娃》，伦敦：豪斯出版社，2005 年，第 160 页。

6. 简娜·汤普森：《妇女与哲学》，邦杜拉：澳大利亚哲学协会，1986 年。

7. 多萝西·E. 史密斯：《日常世界是有问题的：一种女权主义社会学》，波士顿：东北大学出版社，1987 年。

8. 玛丽·斯蓬伯格：《文艺复兴时期以来的妇女历史书写》，纽约：帕尔格雷夫麦克米伦出版社，2002 年。

9. 安德里亚·奈：《女权主义理论与人的哲学》，伦敦：劳特利奇出版社，2013 年。

10. 马热丽·柯林斯和克里斯汀·皮尔斯："空洞和黏液：萨特精神分析学中的性别歧视"，《妇女与哲学》，卡罗尔·C. 古尔德和马克思·W. 沃托夫斯基编，纽约：摩羯座出版社，1976 年。

11. 玛格丽特·A. 西蒙斯："《第二性》是波伏娃对萨特存在主义的运用吗？"，第 20 届世界哲学大会论文，马萨诸塞州波士顿，1998 年 8 月 10—15 日；爱德华·富布鲁克和凯特·富布鲁克：《性与哲学：对德·波伏娃和萨特的重新思考》，伦敦：布鲁姆斯伯里出版社，2008 年。

12. 克里斯廷·戴格尔和雅各·戈洛姆：《萨特和波伏娃：影响的问题》，布卢明顿：印第安纳大学出版社，2009 年。

11 当代印迹

要点 ⚷

- 许多当代女权主义者认为，自从德·波伏娃出版《第二性》以来，现代社会对女性的态度并没有发生太大的变化。

- 性别问题以及现代生活如何仍旧试图从女人很小的时候起就构建"何为女人"的观念，这些话题依然能激起男女双方热烈的反应。

- 《第二性》的英文译本是否模糊了德·波伏娃原本的观点？这一疑问依然存在。

地位

很难想象，一个女权主义思想的分支没受过西蒙娜·德·波伏娃《第二性》的影响；该著作要么带来了启发，要么引起了争论。自该书在 1949 年问世以来，女权主义有了很大的发展，但是当代女权主义者的许多主张都源自该书的观点。

娜塔莎·沃尔特*的《活的洋娃娃：性别歧视的回归》（2010）的标题就取自德·波伏娃对女性的描述："了不起的洋娃娃"。[1] 沃尔特在《第二性》的基础上提出，从德·波伏娃的时代以来，西方社会没有发生什么实质性的变化。沃尔特斯审视了过去半个世纪的发展，以表明 20 世纪 60 年代后女权主义第二次浪潮的影响是短暂的。女性解放已经成为穿着性感和随意性交的权利的同义词，而不是在工作场所或政治领域获得平等的地位。德·波伏娃在《第二性》中表达的恐惧，即女性主义很容易被重新纳入父权制的叙事之中，得到了沃尔特的共鸣。[2] 所以，当俄罗斯女权主义团体"造反猫咪"*的成员将赤裸上身作为一种令人震惊的策略进行抗议时，她们实际上只是落入了男性的注视之中。她们所传递的信息无人听见，原因就在于旁观者关注的只是她们的乳房。

德·波伏娃的观点也影响了朱迪斯·巴特勒 1990 年的力作《性别麻烦》。[3] 巴特勒想了解性别认同和性行为是如何被定义的，她同意德·波伏娃的观点，即性别不具有生物性，而是由文化和社会强加的。然而，虽然德·波伏娃认为父权社会视妇女为缺失的或不存在的，但是巴特勒认为本就不存在性别这种东西，甚至对男性和女性的生殖器进行区别也是错误的，因为我们的理解是基于社会规范的。这就是说，我们对男性和女性生殖器的差异及其内涵的理解本身就是由社会建构的。巴特勒引起争议的著作以重要的新形式发展了波伏娃的观点，促使我们重新思考我们对生理和性别的理解。

> "是建立在私有财产基础上的社会制度导致了对已婚妇女的监护权，是男人取得的技术进步解放了今天的妇女。"
>
> —— 西蒙娜·德·波伏娃:《第二性》

互动

德·波伏娃的著作仍然与公众的争论有关，从女孩如何被指示要穿粉红色的服装到网络游戏世界里的性别歧视。例如，有人发起运动质疑儿童服装和玩具所体现的性别偏见，其中包括"厌恶粉色运动"。他们的运动提醒人们关注那些主要强调外观、时尚和购物的玩具如何造成破坏性影响，严重限制了女孩的志向。这些观点与佩吉·奥伦斯坦和丽贝卡·海恩斯各自的著作《灰姑娘吃了我的女儿》（2011）和《公主问题》（2014）不谋而合。这两本书探讨了市场如何通过将商品分为"男孩专用"和"女孩专用"两类，在损害孩子的情况下去增加利润。[4]

像德·波伏娃一样，当代女权主义者经常面临激烈的批评。"厌恶粉色运动"的创始人收到了来自世界各地的仇恨邮件。劳拉·贝茨*的"每日性别歧视推特活动"（http://everydaysexism.com/）邀请妇女分享她们遭受性别歧视的经历。贝茨遭到了男性权利团体的严厉批评，他们认为这个活动夸大了社会上性别歧视的程度。2014年，在一场占据全球新闻头条的言辞尖刻的运动中，针对电子游戏行业的厌女症（对女性的讨厌或痛恨）的批评家们受到了大量的死亡威胁。这一"游戏丑闻"反映了流行文化展现女性的方式一直存在问题。与此同时，卡洛琳·克里亚多-佩雷斯*在2014年发起了一项运动，目的是使一名妇女的肖像出现在英国钞票上，这场运动最终使得简·奥斯汀的肖像登上了面值10英镑的纸币，但也导致克里亚多-佩雷斯在推特上受到了死亡威胁。

这些强烈的反应表明，对性别身份和性行为的态度在今天仍能引起和在《第二性》刚出版时一样高涨的个人感受，这说明德·波伏娃开启的运动尚未完成。如果要说这两个时间段有什么不同的话，那就是社交媒体所赋予的匿名状态给在数字媒体领域发起运动的女权主义活动者带来了一系列新的挑战。潜在的网上骚扰、跟踪和虐待可能会带来风险，使得互联网转变成又一个限制女性行为、阻止女性发声的空间。

持续争议

《第二性》对于性别研究、酷儿研究和女权主义批评而言十分重要。对于当代学者来说，《第二性》因其历史性和全球性的影响仍具研究价值。1983 年，当女权主义批评家玛格丽特·A.西蒙斯发表了一篇题为"西蒙娜·德·波伏娃的沉默"的重要文章时，《第二性》再次成为人们关注的焦点。西蒙斯详细阐述了法文原著和 H. M. 帕什利的英文译本之间的差异。帕什利遗漏了原著十分之一到三分之一的内容，而且他是一位没有哲学和历史学背景的动物学家。西蒙斯认为，帕什利未能胜任这项翻译工作，并且误译了该书的几个核心的哲学概念。他使用男性主导的表达方式来翻译，极大地破坏了德·波伏娃的女权主义观点。例如，他把"humanité"（人类）翻译为"mankind"（人类；男性），而不是"humankind"（人类），把"le soi"（自我）翻译为"man"（人；男人），而不是"self"（自我）。

西蒙斯的文章披露的事实使一些学者质疑，人们以前基于帕什利的译本对《第二性》作出的评价是否可信。[5]《第二性》新的英文译本在 2009 年出版，接着扩展版译本在 2012 年出版，但这些新译本又引起了新的问题。女权主义作家托里·莫伊曾经指出，德·波伏娃的存在主义观点在该书的第一个译本中被曲解，如今她对该书的新译本感到震惊，她声称其中有许多遗漏、句法错误和误译。[6]

---

1. 西蒙娜·德·波伏娃：《第二性》，H. M. 帕什利译，纽约：艾尔弗雷德·A. 克诺夫出版社，1953 年，第 304 页。

2. 娜塔莎·沃尔特：《活的洋娃娃：性别歧视的回归》，伦敦：维拉戈出版社，2010 年，第 129 页。

3. 朱迪斯·巴特勒："西蒙娜·德·波伏娃《第二性》中的性和性别"，《耶鲁法语研究》，1986 年第 72 期，第 35—49 页；《性别麻烦——女权主义与身份的颠覆》，伦敦：劳特利奇出版社，1990 年，第 11、13、190 页。

4. 佩吉·奥伦斯坦：《灰姑娘吃了我的女儿：来自新女孩文化前线的加急报告》，纽约：哈珀柯林斯出版集团，2011 年；丽贝卡·海恩斯：《公主问题：引导我们的女孩度过痴迷公主的岁月》，伊利诺伊州内伯威尔市：资料读物出版社，2014 年。

5. 玛格丽特·A.西蒙斯："西蒙娜·德·波伏娃的沉默"，《女性研究国际论坛》第 6 卷，1983 年第 5 期，第 559—664 页。

6. 托里·莫伊："淫妇"，《伦敦书评》第 32 卷，2010 年 2 月 11 日第 3 期，登录日期 2015 年 2 月 2 日，https://www.lrb.co.uk/n03/toril-moi/the-adulteress-wife。

12 未来展望

要点 ⚷

- 西蒙娜·德·波伏娃的《第二性》至今仍在激励人们思考和撰文研究性别、身份及女权主义。
- 人们正在将德·波伏娃的观点应用到包括政治学在内的有趣的新领域。
- 《第二性》对现代社会及其对妇女的态度产生了巨大且不可否认的影响。

潜力

西蒙娜·德·波伏娃在《第二性》中宣称，"一个女人不是天生的，而是后天造就的"，[1] 这成为20世纪70年代女权主义活动者的一个战斗口号。今天，在讨论性别认同和性取向的起源时，这仍然是一个强有力的观点。德·波伏娃当时的一些激进的想法——女人应该能够工作或者选择不要孩子——如今在西方文化中已被接受。同样，心理学家和女权主义理论家对诸如"阳具妒羡理论"之类的精神分析学概念的质疑——因为他们发现这些说法并没有什么依据——也证明她是正确的。事实上，该理论本身已经导致许多女权主义者从总体上远离精神分析学，他们认为该理论体现了精神分析学根深蒂固的厌女症。

然而，《第二性》仍然有很多内容可以启发当代人对性别和性行为进行探讨。与20世纪70年代和80年代的女权主义者相比，21世纪的女权主义者可能觉得《第二性》的用处更大。酷儿理论和性别研究的出现使人们重新关注德·波伏娃，原因就在于这些研究也质疑我们定义性别和性取向的方式。德·波伏娃的中心观点是，女性气质是意识形态压迫的工具，女性身份本身也是一种社会建构，而这一观点获得了新的研究价值。

玛丽亚姆·穆塔迈迪－弗雷泽*的《没有自我的身份：西蒙娜·德·波伏娃和双性恋》（1999）就是一个例证，说明了德·波伏娃的理论是如何成为当代有关性别的讨论的一部分的。[2]穆塔迈迪－弗雷泽研究了有关波伏娃的传记、媒体和学术报道，以展示西方关于身份和性行为的观念是如何影响对德·波伏娃著作的学术阐释的。穆塔迈迪－弗雷泽指出，德·波伏娃的性关系和她有关性行为的论述比学者们想象得更加复杂和微妙。该书探讨人们对性取向的文化理解如何影响学术研究——以及会如何导致错误的阐释。

托里·莫伊的《西蒙娜·德·波伏娃：一位知识女性的塑造》（1993）和《何为女性？》（1999）审视了德·波伏娃与整个女权运动有关的女性气质的观点，并且展示了几十年来相互矛盾的理论如何使德·波伏娃的观点难以理解。[3]玛格丽特·A.西蒙斯的《波伏娃与第二性：女权主义、种族与存在主义的起源》（1999）开启了关于女权主义、反殖民主义和人权活动之间的关联的讨论。[4]德·波伏娃的著作在有关发展中国家妇女权利的讨论中有更大的应用潜力。德·波伏娃主张父权制社会认为妇女"不是男人"，与此相呼应，沙曼·琳内特·莫诺根明确论述了父权制价值观在女性割礼的传统中所起的作用。[5]

> "我们生活在一个过渡的时期；这个世界一直属于男人，如今仍然在他们的掌控之中：在很大程度上，父权文明的制度和价值观仍然存在着。"
>
> —— 西蒙娜·德·波伏娃：《第二性》

未来方向

伊丽莎白·法莱兹*、托里·莫伊和玛格丽特·西蒙斯是有影响力的德·波伏娃的拥护者。她们的著作考察了德·波伏娃在女权主义思想史和存在主义传统中的影响。最近,鲁思·埃文斯*、埃莉诺·奥尔韦克、厄休拉·蒂德、索尼亚·克鲁克斯和埃米莉·格罗索兹加入了她们的行列。这些人都对德·波伏娃在人文和社会科学领域中知名度的提高起到了推动作用。

奥尔韦克的《西蒙娜·德·波伏娃的人生体验哲学》(2002)通过研究德·波伏娃的小说和哲学著作审视其存在主义思想。该书把《第二性》与德·波伏娃在职业生涯早期撰写的哲学论文联系起来,以崭新的方法对《第二性》予以阐释。[6] 蒂德的《西蒙娜·德·波伏娃》(2004)对德·波伏娃的所有著作进行了重新解读。[7] 格罗索兹的《西蒙娜·德·波伏娃的遗产》(2006)阐述了德·波伏娃对后来的女权主义思想的影响。[8] 克鲁克斯的《西蒙娜·德·波伏娃与模糊政治学》(2012)将德·波伏娃的著作应用到政治学领域——这是一个鲜有人探索的领域,而克鲁克斯发现,在讨论妇女的政治角色这方面,该领域成果丰硕。[9] 这些著作都证明了德·波伏娃著作一直具有现实意义,也证明了随后的文化转向给该书带来了新的诠释空间。

小结

《第二性》是有关历史上妇女受过的压迫的一项重要研究,也是妇女解放的一个关键时刻。德·波伏娃向我们确切地展现了性别歧视如何渗透到现代社会中,又如何在历史中演变以确保女性保持顺从的状态。通过对有关女性气质的流行观念进行阐释和调查，以及对女性在社会和经济上依赖男性的状态进行分析，德·波伏娃为 20 世纪 60 年代至 70 年代性革命期间女权主义的第二次浪潮铺平了道路。当今，她的著作还被用来探讨性别认同和性取向问题。

21 世纪的读者可能会认为德·波伏娃的观点已经过时或者显而易见。不过，即使德·波伏娃的一些行动呼吁似乎已经过时（例如，女性应该工作），这部著作本身仍然极具现实意义。她对文化神话的影响的审视、她对儿童成长受到"女性气质"看法影响的研究，以及她对性别和性行为的传统定义的质疑，使得她的分析仍然具有强大的影响力。

当然，《第二性》因其历史重要性而与众不同。这是一本引发法国女权运动的著作。正如我们今天所知，德·波伏娃推动了性革命和女权主义的诞生。正如伊丽莎白·巴丹泰在德·波伏娃的墓志铭中所评论的一样："女人们，你们的一切都归功于她！"[10]

---

1. 西蒙娜·德·波伏娃：《第二性》，H. M. 帕什利译，纽约：艾尔弗雷德·A. 克诺夫出版社，1953 年，第 249 页。

2. 玛里亚姆·穆塔迈迪－弗雷泽：《没有自我的身份：西蒙娜·德·波伏娃和双性恋》，剑桥：剑桥大学出版社，1999 年。

3. 托里·莫伊：《西蒙娜·德·波伏娃：一位知识女性的塑造》，牛津和纽约：牛津大学出版社，1993 年；《何为女性？》，牛津和纽约：牛津大学出版社，1999 年。

4. 玛格丽特·A.西蒙斯:《波伏娃与第二性:女性主义、种族与存在主义的起源》,马里兰州拉纳姆和牛津:罗曼和利特菲尔德出版社,1999年。

5. 沙曼·琳内特·莫诺根:"父权制:延续女性割礼的习俗",《国际艺术与人文期刊》第37卷,2010年,第83—99页。

6. 埃莉诺·奥尔韦克:《西蒙娜·德·波伏娃的人生体验哲学》,纽约:罗曼和利特菲尔德出版社,2002年。

7. 厄休拉·蒂德:《西蒙娜·德·波伏娃》,伦敦:劳特利奇出版社,2004年。

8. 埃米莉·格罗索兹:《西蒙娜·德·波伏娃的遗产》,牛津:牛津大学出版社,2006年。

9. 索尼亚·克鲁克斯:《西蒙娜·德·波伏娃与模糊政治学》,牛津:牛津大学出版社,2012年。

10. 引自迪尔德丽·贝尔:《西蒙娜·德·波伏娃传记》,伦敦:岬角出版社,1991年,第617页。

术语表

1. **异化**：个人与其团体的疏离。该术语常与卡尔·马克思的社会异化理论有关，该理论认为异化是财富和权力分配不均的结果。

2. **美国民权运动**：在美国发生的为黑人争取平等权利的运动，包括促使种族隔离制度被宣布为非法和消除已有的针对黑人的歧视性法规。该运动在 20 世纪 50 年代中期产生了一定的影响，在 60 年代达到高潮。

3. **人类学**：研究人类、人类行为及其文化的学科。该学科借鉴了自然、生物、社会和人类科学等许多其他学科。

4. **反殖民主义**：被殖民者或外部团体对殖民主义和殖民统治这一体系的批判或反对。被殖民者或者外部团体认为，该体系在社会上或经济上不公正。

5. **反犹太主义**：基于犹太人的种族、信仰和 / 或文化遗产，对犹太人怀有的偏见、恐惧和歧视。

6. **自主性**：指行为或信仰的独立和自由。一个有自主权的个体能够有合乎自己意愿的信仰和行为。

7. **女学究**：这一术语被用于描述受过教育的知识女性，产生于 18 世纪，但是在 19 世纪被赋予了消极意义，演变成用于指古板的或没有吸引力的女书呆子。

8. **资产阶级**：马克思主义理论中的一个术语，表示拥有生产工具的富裕阶层（例如，生产产品或者提供服务的店主、工厂主或任何其他实体）。

9. **资本主义**：一种生产模式和经济制度。在这种模式或制度下，工业、贸易和生产工具全部或大部分私有，生产和贸易的目的是为了逐利。

10. **殖民主义**：一个国家被另一个国家统治，统治者（殖民者）和被统

治者（殖民地）之间存在不平等的权力关系，殖民者为了加强自己国家的经济发展而剥削殖民地的资源。

11. **去人性化**：将另一个人或者另一些人妖魔化的系统性过程，使其显得不那么像人，从而不配得到人道的对待。

12. **差异化女权主义**：女权主义的一个分支，该分支提出需要承认男女的差异，并试图赞美女人具有的不同特质。对于差异化女权主义者而言，性别平等不应该建立在"女人的举止像男人的一样"这一假设之上。

13. **嫁妆**：新娘家送给新郎的物品、现金或财产，以便新郎同意供养新娘和夫妻俩可能会有的孩子。

14. **平等主义**：拥护平等待遇的主张，该主张的基础假设是所有人拥有平等的价值和社会地位。

15. **解放**：一个被剥夺了权利的群体获得了社会、经济和/或政治权利或者平等。

16. **存在主义/存在主义的人道主义**：一个哲学分支，强调人类主体在无神的状态下追求自我理解、自我认识和承担责任。

17. **女性割礼**：仪式性地切割或割除女性的部分或全部外生殖器，其目的是通过剥夺其性快感或使其在婚前保持贞洁来控制女人的性欲。

18. **女权主义**：一系列与妇女平权有关的意识形态和运动，主张妇女拥有平等的社会、政治、文化和经济权利，包括在家庭、工作场所、教育和政治上的平等权利。

19. **法国抵抗军**：指那些反对维希政权的人。第二次世界大战期间法国被占领，维希政权便与纳粹勾结。抵抗军的成员秘密发行报纸，向同盟国传递一手消息，并参加游击战。

20. **同性恋权利运动**：指从20世纪70年代至今包括公众抗议、游说和示威游行的一系列事件。同性恋者欲以此为同性恋正名，获得和异性恋同等的结婚权和生育权。

21. **性别关系**：两性在其被设定的社会角色的基础之上所展开的互动关系。

22. **性别研究**：有关两性关系、性别认同和性取向的跨学科学术研究，包括性别和性取向是如何在文化中被认知和 / 或展现的。

23. **黑格尔的辩证法**：一种哲学讨论的形式，包括提出一个人的观点（正题），提供抗辩（反题），然后得出使二者一致的结论（合题）。

24. **历史唯物主义**：是由卡尔·马克思发展的一种历史批评方法，该方法把阶级关系和收入不均联系起来以审视历史。

25. **禁书的索引**：罗马天主教会禁止阅读的书目。教会声称这些书中含有不当内容，多与违背教会规定的性行为或社会行为有关。

26. **无邪少女**：法语词，意思是"天真的"，常用于描述受保护的、幼稚的或者无性经验的少女。

27. **跨学科**：对一个问题、命题或话题的研究，其结合了不同的学科知识、思想学派或理论方法。

28. **犹太人**：一个种族–文化和种族–宗教群体，源于古代中东的以色列人。

29. **拉康的精神分析理论**：由雅克·拉康创立的一个精神分析学分支，研究从早期孩童时期开始的身份的发展。

30. 文学批评：对文学进行的评价、研究和阐释。

31. **马达加斯加起义（1947—1948）**：在法属殖民地马达加斯加发生的反抗法国统治的民族主义运动。该起义遭到法军的残酷镇压，法军对马达加斯加的居民进行了大屠杀、折磨和战时强暴。

32. **马克思主义**：指在 19 世纪政治经济学家卡尔·马克思的著作基础上建立的文化、哲学、社会经济、政治和美学理论解读。马克思主义理论家和著作家关注资本主义体制下社会不平等现象的发展及其对文化和社会的影响。

33. **母系后裔或母系社会**：建立在母系血缘关系上的一种世袭继承形

式。该模式和更为常见的沿袭父亲家庭血缘关系的父系社会模式形成对比。

34. **厌女症**：对女人的厌恶或憎恨的态度和行为，包括对女人的性别歧视、暴力、诋毁，以及把女人当作被动的客体来对待（也就是客体化）。

35. **妇女解放运动**：指 1968 年创立的法国第一次妇女权利运动，旨在获得节育权、堕胎权和平等工作的权利。

36. **神话或文化神话**：源自一种文化的意识形态、信仰或世界观的信念。

37. **自恋**：对自身过分的着迷或关注。

38. **纳粹**：也被称为国家社会党。该党从 1933 年至 1945 年二战末统治德国，这一时期也被称为第三帝国时期。纳粹的意识形态在本质上是法西斯主义、反犹太主义和科学种族主义。

39. **黑人文化认同**：20 世纪 30 年代至 50 年代末的一种文学运动，由居住在巴黎的非洲加勒比黑人作家发起，以抗议法国的殖民统治和法国的文化同化。

40. **物化/客体化**：哲学术语，指一个人被当作物来对待的任何状况。"女性的物化"这一术语常用于对性别的探讨，指女人被当作客体来对待，被认为没有主体性，除了吸引男人之外毫无用处。

41. **过时**：指由于时间的推移而导致一个物体、观念或人进入废弃或不存在现实意义的状态。

42. **他者**：哲学家使用的术语，指与人的自我相分离或者有区别。

43. **父权制或父权社会**：指一种社会制度，在该制度中，男性掌握最高权力，担任政治领导角色，被赋予掌控财产的特权，掌握道德权威，或被赋予控制女眷和孩子的权威。

44. **阳具妒羡理论**：精神分析学家一直使用到 20 世纪 50 年代中期的一个术语。照此理论，女性从童年转化为成年时会意识到男人有阴茎，而她们没有。

45. **哲学**：人文学科的一个领域，研究与现实、知识、存在、理性、语言和价值观等相关的基本的人类问题。

46. **政治学**：社会科学的一个领域，研究政府的政策与政治，以及民族、政府和国家的动态。

47. **无产阶级**：在马克思主义理论中，这一术语用于定义那些通过为资产阶级劳动而获取报酬的劳动阶级。

48. **精神分析学**：由奥地利医生西格蒙德·弗洛伊德创立的一门学科，探讨人内心潜意识的活动，并研究人的发展过程中抑制和欲望的作用。

49. **心理学**：一门学术性和应用型的学科，涉及精神行为和精神作用的研究和治疗。

50. **酷儿理论**：一种批判理论的方法，它对文学和文化中关于性或性别身份的传统观点持质疑或排斥态度。

51. **种族主义**：指因对人与人之间（包括种族和民族）生理差异的认知而产生的歧视和偏见。

52. **罗马天主教会**：最大的基督教教会，也是世界上最古老的宗教机构之一。其教义明令禁止堕胎以及除了家庭自然节育以外的任何避孕。

53. **女权主义的第二次浪潮**：指20世纪60年代兴起的妇女权利运动，与性革命同时发生，持续至20世纪80年代晚期。与女权主义的第一次浪潮不同的是，这一时期的妇女主要争取性解放、堕胎合法化和同工同酬。

54. **性别歧视**：基于人的性别的歧视或偏见，可能包括认为一个人低人一等，或因其性别而对其作出某些设想。

55. **性学**：关于人类性行为的研究，包括性方面的兴趣、功能和举止。

56. **性革命**：20世纪60年代至80年代遍及美国和欧洲的一场运动。该运动摒弃涉及性和性规范的传统社会准则与习俗，促进了婚前性行为和避孕的正常化以及许多国家堕胎的合法化。

57. **社会建构**：由社会对群体进行分类或界定的任何类别或定义。社会建构常常给予某一特定群体特权，使其凌驾于其他群体之上，例如男人凌驾于女人之上，或者一个种族凌驾于另一个种族之上。

58. **社会主义革命**：指推翻资本主义、建立社会主义政府的革命，它使社会结构发生变化，包括重新分配社会财富和消灭社会不平等。

59. **社会化**：人类相互学习的过程，包括但不限于吸收信仰体系，学习特别的行为模式，发展与性别、种族或者性行为有关的观点。

60. **社会学**：研究社会行为的学科，该学科研究社会关系的起源和发展、社会组织的不同模式和不同的社会制度。

61. **苏联**：1922年至1991年存在的一个一党制的马克思列宁主义国家，由东欧15个社会主义共和国组成，包括俄罗斯、格鲁吉亚和乌克兰等。

62. **征服**：征服和控制某人或某物，使其屈从。

63. **妇女参政论者**：指19世纪晚期和20世纪早期的争取投票权的妇女。

64. **《驯悍记》**（1590—1593）：莎士比亚的一部剧作，讲述了一个男人对一个强势反叛的女人（即"悍妇"）的系统驯化。

65. **《摩登时代》**：由让-保罗·萨特和西蒙娜·德·波伏娃于1945年创办的左翼刊物，根据查理·卓别林的电影《摩登时代》而命名。

66. **维希政权**（1940—1944）：第二次世界大战期间，法国向纳粹德国投降后在法国建立的一个临时政体，它和纳粹政府沆瀣一气。

67. **《妇女与社会主义》**：一部历史著作，描述女性从史前到19世纪末遭受的压迫，作者是德国的社会主义者奥古斯特·倍倍尔，他认为女性解放是社会主义成功的关键。

68. **女权运动**：为使妇女获得和男性同等的权利而进行的一系列行动。该运动的发生具有阶段性，不同国家在不同时期赢得了妇女权利，但是人们普遍认为，该运动在20世纪60年代晚期和70年代早期达到了顶峰。

69. **妇女研究**：研究性别、性、阶级、种族和国家地位的跨学科研究，提出女性身份是这些因素共同作用的结果。该学科于 20 世纪 70 年代在美国兴起，受到女权主义第二次浪潮的极大影响。

70. **第二次世界大战**（1939—1945）：在英国、法国、苏联、美国等国家与德国、意大利和日本之间展开的一场战争。

人名表

1. **伊丽莎白·巴丹泰**（1944 年生），法国历史学家、作家，巴黎综合理工学院哲学教授，以其女权主义著作而闻名，包括备受争议的《冲突、妇女与母亲身份》（2010）。

2. **约翰·巴霍芬**（1815—1887），德国人类学家、作家，以其"史前和近代社会是母系社会"的观点而著名。他认为母系社会给了妇女更多的权力。

3. **劳拉·贝茨**，英国女权主义活动家和新闻记者，以其发起的"日常性别歧视"运动而著称，该运动旨在提高对妇女日常所经历的性别歧视的关注。

4. **奥古斯特·倍倍尔**（1840—1913），德国社会主义作家和政治家，以其著作《女性与社会主义》（1879）而闻名。

5. **黛布拉·伯格芬**，美国大学"汉密尔顿主教"哲学讲师、乔治·梅森大学哲学荣誉教授，主要成果涉及当代哲学思想、女权主义理论和人权。

6. **安德烈·布莱顿**（1896—1966），法国作家、诗人和视觉艺术家，20 世纪早期的激进艺术运动"超现实主义"的奠基人之一。他最著名的作品也许是他的小说《娜嘉》（1928）和《疯狂的爱》（1937）。

7. **朱迪斯·巴特勒**（1956 年生），女权主义者、酷儿理论和性别关系学者，以著作《性别麻烦》（1990）而闻名。在这部著作中，她提出性别纯粹是一种社会建构，与生理或者身体方面的事实完全分离。

8. **阿尔贝·加缪**（1913—1960），法国小说家、剧作家、存在主义哲学家和新闻记者，在 1957 年获得诺贝尔文学奖。

9. **埃莱娜·西苏**（1937 年生），法国著名女权主义诗人、哲学家和文学评论家，以其女权主义名著《美杜莎的笑声》（1975）而闻名。在这部著作中，她规劝女性读者摆脱现代语言的阳具中心主义，采纳她所谓的"女性写作"(阴性书写)。

10. 保罗·克洛岱尔(1868—1955),法国诗人、剧作家。德·波伏娃在《第二性》中激烈地批评了他对女性的歧视性描述。

11. 卡洛琳·克里亚多-佩雷斯(1984年生),英国新闻记者和女权主义活动家。她因竭力主张应当允许女性在英国媒体上更好地展现自己以及钞票上应当印制女性肖像而闻名。后一项运动促使英格兰银行决定在2017年前将简·奥斯汀的肖像印制到10英镑纸币上。

12. 克里斯廷·戴格尔,加利福尼亚布鲁克大学的哲学教授,专门研究欧洲大陆传统的存在主义、现象学和女权主义理论。

13. 弗里德里希·恩格斯(1820—1895),德国哲学家,卡尔·马克思的亲密战友,和马克思合著了《共产党宣言》(1848)。他的《家庭起源、私有财产与国家》(1884)给德·波伏娃带来了许多灵感,如今被女权主义学者视为一部重要的著作。

14. 鲁思·埃文斯,密苏里州圣路易斯大学的"多萝西·麦克布莱德·奥斯文"教授,主要研究中世纪英语文学(1300—1580)和女权主义理论与批评。

15. 伊丽莎白·法莱兹(1950—2009),英国学者、女权主义者,法国研究的领军人物,西蒙娜·德·波伏娃著作研究的国际权威。她的研究包括德·波伏娃的小说和哲学著作。

16. 安托瓦内特·富克(1936—2014),法国精神分析学家、女权主义活动家,1968年法国"妇女解放运动"的发起人之一,被认为是法国最卓越的女权主义者之一。

17. 凯特·富布鲁克(1951—2003),出生于美国的学者,以在英国参加争取自由教育的运动而闻名,还以评论女权主义理论、女性创作的现代主义小说以及西蒙娜·德·波伏娃和萨特的关系而闻名。

18. 格奥尔格·威廉·弗里德里希·黑格尔(1770—1831),德国哲学家、唯心主义运动的主要代表人物,以其对现实的历史主义和现实主义论述而著名。他提出心灵与自然、主体与客体等因素存在于一个密不可分的"系统"之内,而"系统"是最早承认矛盾与对立共存于一个体系之内的概念之一。

19. **露丝·伊利格瑞**（1930 年生），生于比利时的法国女权主义哲学家、语言学家和文化理论家，最著名的著作是《他者女人的窥镜》（1974）和《非一之性别》（1977）。

20. **菲奥纳·詹金斯**，澳大利亚国立大学哲学系高级讲师，主要研究当代法国哲学。

21. **阿尔弗雷德·金赛**（1894—1956），美国生物学家、动物学教授，以其性学领域的开创性工作而著名，他的主要观点记载在他的著作《男性中的性行为》（1948）和《女性中的性行为》（1953）中。

22. **朱莉娅·克里斯蒂娃**（1941 年生），保加利亚裔法国女权主义哲学家、精神分析学家和文学批评家，以其著作《恐怖的力量》（1982）、《女性时间》（1981）和《黑太阳》（1992）而闻名。

23. **雅克·拉康**（1901—1981），法国精神分析学家和精神病学家，因发展了拉康精神分析理论而闻名，该理论对法国哲学和女权主义理论产生了深远影响。

24. **D. H. 劳伦斯**（1885—1930），英国小说家、短篇小说家和散文家，因小说《查泰莱夫人的情人》（1928）而闻名。多年来该小说因露骨的性描写而被删节。

25. **米歇尔·勒德夫**（1948 年生），法国哲学家、女权主义作家，以其《希帕契亚的选择：一篇关于女性、哲学以及其他的论文》（1991）和《知之性》（1998）而闻名。

26. **克劳德·列维-施特劳斯**（1908—2009），法国民族学家和人类学家，常被誉为"现代人类学之父"。

27. **伊莱恩·马克斯**（1930—2001），法国文学、女权主义理论和妇女写作的权威专家，因其关于西蒙娜·德·波伏娃和科莱特的开创性论著而著名。

28. **卡尔·马克思**（1818—1883），德国政治哲学家和经济学家，其有关资本主义制度下阶级关系的分析和有关更为平等的制度的论述为共产主义奠定了基础。

29. **弗朗索瓦·莫里亚克**（1885—1970），法国小说家，1952年诺贝尔文学奖获得者。然而，他因小说中含有歧视女性的观点而受到批判。

30. **托里·莫伊**（1953年生），生于挪威的美国女权主义作家和德·波伏娃研究者，她的多部著作论述德·波伏娃在法国和美国的女权运动中所发挥的作用，包括《性/文本政治》（1985）、《西蒙娜·德·波伏娃：一位知识女性的塑造》（1994）以及《何为女性？及其他论文》（1999）。

31. **刘易斯·亨利·摩根**（1818—1881），美国人类学家和社会主义理论家。他最为著名的论断是：最早的家庭制度（家庭）是基于母系建立的，家庭成员都以母系来确认，后代也按照母系来追溯。

32. **玛丽亚姆·穆塔迈迪－弗雷泽**，伦敦大学金史密斯学院社会学的准教授，因其有关以色列和中东、女权主义理论以及性方面的论著而闻名。

33. **亨利·德·蒙特朗**（1895—1972），法国作家，因其厌恶女性的观点而著名，体现此类观点的代表作是他的反女权主义四部曲系列小说《少女们》。德·波伏娃在《第二性》中花费了整整一章的篇幅来探讨蒙特朗的反女权主义立场。

34. **安德里亚·奈**（1939年生），女权主义作家、哲学家，因其女权主义哲学著作而闻名，包括《权力话语：对逻辑史的女权主义解读》（1990）和《女权主义与现代哲学导论》（2004）。

35. **朱迪思·奥凯利**（1941年生），英国赫尔大学的社会学和人类学名誉教授，因其关于西蒙娜·德·波伏娃的论著和关于身份、自传和人类学实践的著作而闻名。

36. **卡米尔·帕利亚**（1947年生），美国社会批评家、学者和"持不同政见的"女权主义者。她闻名的原因在于她对女权主义学者和妇女研究的尖锐批评、她在许多女权主义问题上有争议的立场以及她对西蒙娜·德·波伏娃的崇拜。

37. **H. M. 帕什利**（1884—1953），《第二性》的第一位译者。有人批评他的英文翻译删减了原著的重要部分，对于某些词汇的翻译体现和延续了德·波伏娃著作中所批判的男性中心主义思想，比如他把"human"（人）翻译成"man"（人；男人），把"humankind"（人类）译成"mankind"（人类；男性）。

38. 造反猫咪，俄罗斯的一个女权主义朋克乐队。她们经常用音乐抗议对女性的压迫和本国政府的领导。

39. 凯瑟琳·罗杰斯，威尔士斯旺西大学语言、翻译和交流方面的副教授。她对法国当代女性写作、女权主义理论、玛格丽特·杜拉斯和西蒙娜·德·波伏娃的作品进行评论。

40. 让-保罗·萨特（1905—1980），法国卓越的存在主义哲学家，德·波伏娃的终身伴侣和同事。他的作品深受"人注定是自由的"和"没有造物主"这些观念的影响。

41. 威廉·莎士比亚（1564—1616），英国剧作家、演员和诗人，被认为是有史以来最杰出的英语作家。他的剧作包括《罗密欧与朱丽叶》《麦克白》《李尔王》和《驯悍记》。

42. 玛格丽特·A.西蒙斯，美国女权主义哲学家和批评家。她写了大量关于德·波伏娃和女权主义批评的著作。

43. 多萝西·E.史密斯（1926年生），加拿大社会学家、女权主义者和妇女研究理论家，是女权主义立场理论（该理论认为权威源自个人的知识）和建制民族志（该理论在诸如工作场所之类的社会组织内规划个人的关系）这两个社会学分支学科的创建人之一。

44. 玛丽·斯蓬伯格，主要研究女权主义理论、现代历史和妇女历史的澳大利亚学者，国际刊物《澳大利亚女权主义研究》的编辑，《女性化的性病》（1995）的作者。

45. 约瑟夫·斯大林（1878—1953），1917年俄罗斯革命的领导人之一。他从20世纪20年代中期至1953年去世前担任苏联的领导人。

46. 司汤达（1783—1842），马里-亨利·贝尔的笔名，19世纪法国作家，因其小说《巴马修道院》（1893）和《红与黑》（1830）而闻名。

47. **简娜·汤普森**，澳大利亚拉筹伯大学的哲学教授。她的作品涉及政治哲学、人权、女权主义理论和伦理学。

48. **娜塔莎·沃尔特**（1967年生），女权主义作家和活动家，因其著作《新女权主义》（1998）和《活玩偶：性别歧视的回归》（2010）而闻名。

49. **内奥米·沃尔夫**（1962年生），当代女权主义批评家、新闻记者和作家，因领导其后来所称的女权主义第三次浪潮及其作品《美丽的神话》（1991）而闻名。

50. **玛莉·渥斯顿克雷福特**（1759—1797），英国哲学家、作家。她提倡妇女的权利，因其《为女权辩护》而闻名，在该著作中，她支持妇女的受教育权。

51. **弗吉尼亚·伍尔芙**（1882—1944），英国小说家和散文家，以其创新的实验性写作风格和有关女性的激进观点而闻名。她因小说《达洛维夫人》（1925）、《奥兰多》（1928）及女权主义散文《一间自己的房间》（1929）而闻名。

WAYS IN TO THE TEXT

- Simone de Beauvoir was a radical French philosopher and writer.

- *The Second Sex* was an analysis of why women have always had less power and freedom than men.

- De Beauvoir drew on different disciplines to argue that women have been oppressed throughout history, and her book helped to set the feminist* movement in motion.

Who Was Simone de Beauvoir?

Simone de Beauvoir was a radical French philosopher, writer, and political activist whose groundbreaking work tackled the underdog status of women and inspired the feminist movement.

Born in 1908, de Beauvoir grew up in a middle-class Parisian family and was a gifted scholar. Her father was a lawyer who encouraged his daughter to study, while her mother was a devout Roman Catholic. At convent school de Beauvoir considered becoming a nun, but later came to be an atheist and remained one for the rest of her life.

In 1929 she earned a degree in philosophy* at the Paris Sorbonne—also known as Paris University. De Beauvoir was one of only a handful of female graduates. When she was 21 she met the philosopher Jean-Paul Sartre* at the renowned École Normale Supérieure and they were lovers and friends until his death in 1980. De Beauvoir became a secondary school teacher but was suspended from teaching after a scandal involving accusations that she and Sartre had seduced one of her female students in 1939.

De Beauvoir published her first novel, *She Came to Stay*

(based on the scandal), in 1943, and her first philosophical essay, *Pyrrhus and Cinéas*, in 1944. Next came *The Ethics of Ambiguity* (1947) and *The Second Sex* (1949). Her semi-autobiographical novel *The Mandarins* followed in 1954.[1]

In 1972 de Beauvoir declared herself a feminist, revising her previous stance that a socialist revolution* would be enough to emancipate* women.[2] She died of pneumonia in 1986 and is buried beside Sartre in the cemetery of Montparnasse in Paris.

What Does *The Second Sex* Say?

De Beauvoir's book tackles women's social status from the beginning of civilization to the modern day. Her central argument is that women have been forced to take a secondary role to men since the earliest times, and that the whole human condition is viewed in male terms and is described in language that excludes women.

De Beauvoir makes her case using three frames of reference. The first is historical materialism,* which addresses the influence of social and economic conditions and class on shaping history. De Beauvoir also employs existentialism*—the philosophy that emphasizes personal freedom and choice in a world where there is no God or other higher power. Then she brings psychoanalysis* to bear in examining the underlying (known as "subconscious") causes of human behavior.

De Beauvoir's historical materialist investigation shows how women have been trapped into dependence on men in every area of their lives, ensuring they have no real power in culture or society.

She highlights how society treated women as legal minors, very like children. This frustrated their ability to take part in public life on an equal footing with men. For these reasons, women are largely absent from the great stories of history. Men have always been granted greater economic, political, and social power, so they have also had more influence on cultural and historical events.[3]

Viewing the female lot through an existentialist lens, de Beauvoir argues that femininity is constructed. By this she means that a person's nature depends on outside forces. This is the complete opposite of the traditional philosophical view that human nature is fixed at birth. As an existentialist, de Beauvoir argues that human beings are not born with any particular values and create an identity only as a result of their circumstances. *The Second Sex* famously states that no one is born a woman, but rather becomes one through how she is raised and treated by society.

Throughout history, de Beauvoir argues, women have been cast as the "Other."* This is a philosopher's term for that which is separate or distinct from the human self. De Beauvoir argues that society views women as the "Other," because they are viewed only in relation to men. They are treated as objects of desire for men, as mothers to their future heirs, or as the ones who look after everyone else. Denying women their own subjectivity (the right to view themselves as individuals) with their own perspective is dehumanizing* and leaves them powerless.

Psychoanalysis is used in *The Second Sex* to expose the contradictions and untruths in myths* about femininity that are to be found throughout art, literature, religion, and popular culture. De

Beauvoir argues that cultural understandings of femininity have no basis in fact. Instead they are rooted in male fear and male desire. They express men's longing to possess, own, and achieve in the world. Women's sole purpose in society is to satisfy such male longings. The female role in these myths is passive. Without men pursuing them, seducing them, or making them their wives, women have no reason to exist.

Why Does *The Second Sex* Matter?

The Second Sex is a milestone in the study of women's experience in society and is regarded by some as marking the birth of feminism. De Beauvoir's resounding achievement was to show the full extent of the sexism* at work in modern society. Her broad vision and use of critical tools from several disciplines were put to work methodically in making her case across all areas of literature, culture, and scholarship.

De Beauvoir tackled head on the accepted, centuries-old beliefs about women's place in the home and the function of marriage. She questioned the very idea of femininity. The book stirred up a storm of controversy in the conservative France of 1949, and de Beauvoir was criticized and ridiculed both for her ideas and her private life. However, *The Second Sex* set decades of debate in motion about patriarchical* (male-centered) attitudes that endures to this day.

It is also true that to a twenty-first century reader, many of de Beauvoir's theories may seem to be stating the obvious. Radical books like *The Second Sex* are often doomed to having their ideas seem dated to future generations. By calling the status quo into question, the book helped to bring about change. That some parts of the text have become obsolete* could be regarded as achieving the desired result. This means aspects of de Beauvoir's analysis will feel out of date and some of her demands (such as her call for all women to work) may have been overtaken by questions about how it is possible to both work and raise children.

At the same time, de Beauvoir's work as a whole remains intensely relevant to modern debate. *The Second Sex* is still consulted for its contribution to core areas of academic and social concern. These include de Beauvoir's emphasis on how male power is built on cultural myths*. And the messages society feeds girls about femininity is still a matter for concern more than half a century after she first identified the problem.

The work is still a highly original approach to how we define gender and sexual orientation. It also stands alone for its historical importance. This is the text that paved the way for the feminist movement and helped to launch the fight for women's rights in France, the United States, and around the world.

---

1. Simone de Beauvoir, *She Came to Stay*, trans. Roger Senhouse and Yvonne Moyse (New York: W. W. Norton & Co., 1954); *Pyrrhus et Cinéas* (Paris: Gallimard, 1944); *The Ethics of Ambiguity*, trans. Bernard Frechtman (New York: Citadel Press, 1996); *The Mandarins*, trans. Leonard M. Friedman (New York: W. W. Norton & Co., 1991).

2. Elizabeth Fallaize, *Simone de Beauvoir: A Critical Reader* (London: Routledge, 1998), 6.

3. Simone de Beauvoir, *The Second Sex*, trans. H. M. Parshley (New York: Alfred A. Knopf, 1953), 123.

SECTION 1
INFLUENCES

THE AUTHOR AND THE HISTORICAL CONTEXT

KEY POINTS

- *The Second Sex* was written just after World War II* and was a groundbreaking account of women's oppression from the beginning of human history to the present day.
- Both de Beauvoir's intellectual environment and her lover, the philosopher Jean-Paul Sartre,* played a role in shaping the work.
- She was influenced by the anti-colonialist* and American Civil Rights* movements, by postwar discussions about anti-Semitism,* and by the recent gains of French women in the workforce.

Why Read This Text?

The Second Sex by Simone de Beauvoir was first published in 1949 and is regarded as a landmark feminist* manifesto. Its unprecedented analysis of female status throughout history triggered decades of discussion around how sexism* governs the lives of women.

De Beauvoir uses a series of theoretical approaches to tackle the origins and wide-reaching effects of female oppression and the work has been a key text in the women's rights movement.* It is partly thanks to *The Second Sex* that we now acknowledge women's contribution to the workforce and accept that some women do not want children.

De Beauvoir was the first thinker to suggest that a person

was not born with a gender identity but acquired one through the influence of society and culture. This idea is fundamental to the disciplines of queer theory* and gender studies.* De Beauvoir's assertion that "One is not born, but rather becomes a woman" is among the most famous statements in feminist theory.[1]

The Second Sex takes an interdisciplinary* approach to exploring the force of cultural myths* and how ideas about femininity affect child development. The book is an enduring work of scholarship that is still important in the modern debate around the status of women.

> *"What is a woman? ... The fact that I ask it is in itself significant. A man would never get the notion of writing a book on the peculiar situation of the human male. But if I wish to define myself, I must first of all say:'I am a woman'; on this truth must be based all further discussion."*
>
> ——Simone de Beauvoir, *The Second Sex*

Author's Life

Simone de Beauvoir was born in Paris in 1908 and grew up in a wealthy middle-class family. She was raised a Roman Catholic,* but became an atheist at the age of 14. She excelled in her studies and took a degree in philosophy,* becoming one of only nine women to graduate from the famous Sorbonne University in Paris in 1929.

After university, de Beauvoir sat in on courses at the prestigious college for academics and civil servants called the École Normale

Supérieure, even though women had not yet been admitted to the institution. It was here, aged 21, that she met fellow philosopher Jean-Paul Sartre. De Beauvoir went on to teach at a secondary school in the French city of Rouen, and she and Sartre became a couple. De Beauvoir was opposed to marriage and they never had children. They also had an open relationship, which was a controversial arrangement for the time. Scandal erupted when allegations were filed against de Beauvoir for sexual misconduct against a female student. The student's parents accused de Beauvoir and Sartre of acting together to seduce their 17-year-old daughter in 1939.

The allegations—raised much later—led to de Beauvoir being suspended from teaching in 1943. Her first novel, translated in English as *She Came to Stay* (1943), was a fictionalized account of a similar affair. She published her first philosophical essay, *Pyrrhus and Cinéas*, in 1944, and *The Ethics of Ambiguity* in 1947. *The Second Sex* in 1949 was followed by the novel *The Mandarins* in 1954, which won France's most prestigious literary prize, the Prix Goncourt.

De Beauvoir spent her later years writing travel essays and a four-volume autobiography. In 1972 she declared herself a feminist for the first time, revising her earlier claim that a socialist revolution would be enough to liberate women.[2] She campaigned for women's rights both in France and the United States until her death in 1986.

Author's Background

De Beauvoir's work was shaped by the aftermath of World War II and the radical beliefs that fueled a number of different ideas, including Marxism,* existentialism,* and the Civil Rights movement.*

Marxism is a political theory based on the works of the nineteenth-century philosopher and social theorist Karl Marx.* Marx said that by pursuing profit, the economic system of capitalism* created class inequality and encouraged the exploitation of labor. De Beauvoir was influenced by the Marxism of the Soviet Union,* where leader Joseph Stalin* ran a centrally planned economy. Stalin claimed his system eliminated social classes and private property by making all resources public under state control.

Many on the French Left, including de Beauvoir, believed that a socialist revolution* was key to solving postwar France's economic woes. She modeled her idea of female freedom on her perception of women's role in the newly formed Soviet Union.

Existentialism was a philosophical movement made famous by Sartre, de Beauvoir's partner, in the 1940s. It emphasized the existence of the individual, along with freedom of choice. In *Existentialism is a Humanism* (1946), Sartre reversed the traditional idea that a person is born with an identity. He argued instead that "existence precedes essence" and that "man first of all exists, encounters himself, surges up in the world—and defines himself afterwards."[3] He meant that human identity is not fixed and is a product of circumstance. De Beauvoir argued that if identity is socially constructed then femininity is also created the same way.

De Beauvoir believed that existentialism could be used to liberate women. France had only granted women the right to vote in 1944 as more women joined the workforce when men went to fight in World War II. One of her concerns in *The Second Sex* was to cement and build on the powers women had gained during the war.

De Beauvoir's work was also influenced by the French anti-colonialist movement[4] that was fighting to end the oppression of France's minority groups. The Malagasy Uprising* in 1947 raised public awareness of oppression in French colonies. In *The Second Sex* de Beauvoir contrasts the solidarity felt between ethnic minorities fighting their oppressors to the attitude of women, which is actually complicit with their oppressors. She looks at the way women feel more solidarity with their fathers and husbands than they do with other women. For this to change, de Beauvoir says they must switch their loyalty and join together with other women. According to her, without solidarity the fight for women's freedom will fail.

---

1. Simone de Beauvoir, *The Second Sex*, trans. H. M. Parshley (New York: Alfred A. Knopf, 1953), 249.

2. Elizabeth Fallaize, *Simone de Beauvoir: A Critical Reader* (London: Routledge, 1998), 6.

3. Jean-Paul Sartre, "Existentialism and Humanism," in *Jean-Paul Sartre: Basic Writings*, ed. Stephen Priest (New York: Routledge, 2002), 28.

4. Margaret A. Simons, *De Beauvoir and* The Second Sex*: Feminism, Race, and the Origins of Existentialism* (New York: Rowman & Littlefield, 1999).

MODULE 2
ACADEMIC CONTEXT

KEY POINTS

* *The Second Sex* is not confined to a single academic field and in it de Beauvoir draws on history, philosophy* and literature.
* The work tackles human freedom and the role of social structures in creating either freedom or oppression.
* De Beauvoir built her arguments about the role of women by using elements of existential humanism,* Marxist* historical materialism,* and Lacanian psychoanalysis.*

The Work in Its Context

In *The Second Sex*, Simone de Beauvoir takes a broad interdisciplinary approach to her work that draws on philosophy, history, and literary criticism.* This is necessary because a woman's life adds up to more than her sexuality, her biology, or her economic status. In the book she says, "The categories of 'clitorid' [clitoris] and 'vaginal', like the categories of 'bourgeois'* or 'proletarian',* are equally inadequate to encompass a concrete woman."[1]

De Beauvoir's project was highly original. Before *The Second Sex* appeared in 1949, the examination of women in history, culture, and society was glaringly absent. Scholars who addressed the condition of women were largely ignored and were only reclaimed from obscurity by feminist* scholars in the 1970s. These neglected thinkers included the philosopher Mary Wollstonecraft,* the socialist writer August Bebel,* and anthropologists* Johann Jakob Bachoffen* and Lewis Henry Morgan.*

Wollstonecraft's 1792 work *A Vindication of the Rights of Woman* argued that, like men, women should receive an education. Later contributions from Bebel, Bachoffen, and Morgan that specifically addressed the broader social role of women were only recognized when feminist scholarship emerged from the mid-1970s onward.[2] Little attention was paid to Morgan and Bachoffen's claims that prehistoric and early modern societies were based on matrilineal* lines, meaning that people were identified in relation to their mothers.[3]

Before the 1960s few humanities scholars outside of history departments explored the position of women, with the notable exception of English novelist Virginia Woolf.* In her essay *A Room of One's Own* (1929) Woolf argues that Shakespeare's* success was a product not only of his talent but of the freedom he was granted as a man.[4] But like Bebel and the German philosopher and political theorist Friedrich Engels* before her, Woolf's views did little to shift public opinion about women.

> *"The whole of feminine history has been man-made. Just as in America there is no Negro problem, but rather a white problem; just as anti-Semitism* is not a Jewish* problem, it is our problem; so the woman problem has always been man's problem."*
>
> —— Simone de Beauvoir, *The Second Sex*

Overview of the Field

De Beauvoir's historical analysis of women's oppression draws heavily on Marxist historical materialism. This approach to history was developed by the political theorists Karl Marx* and Friedrich Engels and focuses on the role of class struggle, social inequality, and the exploitation of labor. Engels saw the role of women in society through a historical materialist lens. De Beauvoir was inspired by Engels's argument that throughout history women were objects of exchange, or commodities, and that capitalist* ideologies reinforced this. Engels viewed marriage as a series of financial transactions between the bride's father and the groom. Similarly, de Beauvoir's central idea is based on Bebel's argument in *Women and Socialism** that woman "is the first human being which came into servitude. Women were slaves before men."[5]

Engels and Bebel saw women's emancipation*—their gaining of freedom from oppression—as something that would enable a socialist revolution,* but de Beauvoir reversed the equation. For her, a socialist revolution would enable women's emancipation:"A world where men and women would be equal is easy to visualize, for that precisely is what the Soviet* Revolution promised."[6] In other words, where Engels and Marx make women a tool for revolution, de Beauvoir makes revolution a tool for women. But she also argues that historical materialism's ability to explain women's experience is limited by its materialist focus, which "reduc[es] men and women to no more than economic units."[7]

De Beauvoir also developed her ideas in direct opposition to a branch of psychoanalysis*—a system of theory and therapy devoted to understanding the mind—developed by the Frenchman Jacques Lacan.* She took issue with Lacan's concept of the mirror stage. This says children learn to view themselves as fully formed individuals when they recognize their reflection in a mirror. De Beauvoir argued that this is not true for female children as little girls are taught from an early age to look and act in the way others want them to. When a girl looks in the mirror she doesn't see herself; she sees a projection of the expectations of the outside world. These include aspiring to "look like a picture" by "compar[ing] herself to princesses and fairies."[8]

De Beauvoir also challenges the psychoanalytic theory of penis envy.* This holds that female development from childhood to womanhood is marked by a recognition in adolescence that they are lacking a penis. De Beauvoir identified this theory as another male view and argued "these theories themselves should be submitted to psychoanalysis."[9]

Academic Influences

De Beauvoir explains female oppression by using existentialist philosophy to fill the gaps left by historical materialist and psychoanalytic theory. An existentialist approach, she argues, takes into account the "total situation" of women. A woman is "a human being in quest of values in a world of values."[10] In other words, a woman is more than a body or an economic unit.

The central argument of *The Second Sex* is that women are viewed as objects through which men understand the world. De Beauvoir frames this argument in existentialist terms. Existentialism holds that human beings have the capacity to forge their own destinies, and can define themselves on their own terms. De Beauvoir extends this idea to argue that women have the capacity to overcome their secondary status, and define themselves independently from men. In her autobiography de Beauvoir credits Sartre as the inspiration for this approach, but scholars disagree over the extent of his role.[11]

The book also draws on the work of eighteenth-century German philosopher Georg Wilhelm Friedrich Hegel.* He described the human condition as a negotiation between "subject" (the person) and "Other"* (that which is different or alien to the person). De Beauvoir argues that society views humanity purely in male terms and so relegates women to the role of "Other." Women are defined socially and sexually in relation to men and in the way that they are different (or "Other") to men:"Woman ... finds herself living in a world where men compel her to assume the status of the Other."[12]

De Beauvoir used Hegelian dialectic*—that is, putting seemingly contradictory ideas together to reach a higher truth— to show that female identity is constructed negatively. As human beings we regard ourselves as essential because we experience the world in relation to ourselves. But society teaches women that they are *in*essential. She says:"The whole drama of woman lies in this conflict between the aspirations of every subject (ego)— who always regards the self as essential—and the compulsions of a situation in which she is the inessential."[13] Women are perceived as inferior simply because they are not men and that is why society treats a woman as a negative version of a man.

---

1. Simone de Beauvoir, *The Second Sex*, trans. H. M. Parshley (New York: Alfred A. Knopf, 1953), 91.

2. Joan Kelly-Gadol, "The Social Relation of the Sexes: Methodological Implications of Women's History," in *Feminism and Methodology: Social Science Issues,* ed. Sandra G. Harding (Bloomington and Indianapolis: Indiana University Press, 1987), 22.

3. Kelly-Gadol, "The Social Relation of the Sexes," 23.

4. Virginia Woolf, *A Room of One's Own* (London and New York: Penguin, 2002).

5. August Bebel, *Women and Socialism*, trans. Meta L. Stern (New York: Socialist Literature Company and Co-operative Press, 1910 [1879]).

6. De Beauvoir, *The Second Sex*, 652.

7. De Beauvoir, *The Second Sex*, 54.

8. De Beauvoir, *The Second Sex*, 264.

9. De Beauvoir, *The Second Sex*, 221.

10. De Beauvoir, *The Second Sex*, 84.

11. Edward Fullbrook and Kate Fullbrook, *Sex and Philosophy: Re-thinking de Beauvoir and Sartre* (London: Bloomsbury, 2008).

12. De Beauvoir, *The Second Sex*, xxviii.

13. De Beauvoir, *The Second Sex*, xxviii.

MODULE 3
THE PROBLEM

KEY POINTS

- *The Second Sex* was a call to action to scholars and the public to rethink their assumptions about women and their role in society.
- It challenged established ideas in psychoanalysis,* philosophy,* and history to ask a completely new question: what are the causes and effects of female oppression?
- De Beauvoir's open interest in female sexuality was unusual at the time and her own unconventional sex life led to some personal criticism.

Core Question

Simone de Beauvoir did not write *The Second Sex* in response to an existing debate. She wrote it to open up a brand new area of inquiry and asked big questions: What is a woman? When we talk about humanity, why do we say *man*kind?

De Beauvoir wanted to discuss society's very definitions of gender. That meant examining the far-reaching implications of women's secondary status at home, at work, in politics, and in culture generally. Her views on female sexuality and reproduction marked a radical departure from those of contemporary psychologists* and sociologists,* while her ideas on female subjectivity (the freedom to be an individual) were entirely new to philosophy.

De Beauvoir believed that women should play a full part in academic inquiry. She was convinced that allowing the study of the human sciences to be conducted only by the male half of the species leads at best to a skewed understanding of humanity and at worst to major misrepresentation.

In *The Second Sex* De Beauvoir systematically challenges and disproves commonly held notions about women on a social, psychological, and biological level. She even goes so far as to question scientists' assumptions about female anatomy, including the reproductive system and sexual desire. In doing so she opened the door to an entirely new set of questions among scholars and in wider society:"How can a human being in a woman's situation attain fulfillment? What roads are open to her and which are blocked? How can independence be recovered in a state of dependency?"[1]

> "One is not born, but rather becomes, a woman. No biological, psychological, or economic fate determines the figure that the human female presents in society; it is civilization as a whole that produces this creature, intermediate between male and eunuch, which is described as feminine. Only the intervention of someone else can establish an individual as an Other."
>
> ——Simone de Beauvoir, *The Second Sex*

The Participants

The Second Sex challenges established ideas in the fields of psychoanalysis, philosophy, and history. First, de Beauvoir argues that the challenges women face are not internal, as claimed by psychoanalysis. Women's challenges are external and the biggest obstacles to self-fulfillment are to be found in culture and social context."The very language of psychoanalysis suggests that the drama of the individual unfolds within him ... But a life is a relation to the world, and the individual defines himself by making choices through the world about him. We must therefore turn toward the world to find answers."[2]

Second, de Beauvoir does not believe that a woman's destiny is mapped out from childhood. Psychoanalysis lays great emphasis on early events and traumatic memories from which we supposedly cannot escape. Historical materialism,* meanwhile, suggests our path in life is dictated by economic circumstances. De Beauvoir acknowledges the influence of both these factors but argues that women have the power to overcome them. This idea builds on the existentialist* concept of free will."In order to explain her limitations it is woman's situation that must be invoked and not a mysterious essence; thus the future remains largely open."[3]

Third, de Beauvoir challenges the habit of psychoanalysts to relate women's psychological maturity to their anatomy. For example, she challenges psychoanalysts' view that clitoral orgasms (rather than vaginal) are a sign of sexual immaturity.[4] She links the opinion to the fact that a clitoral orgasm can be had without a man and has no reproductive function. Vaginal orgasm "consigns woman to man and childbearing ... put[ting] woman into a state of dependency upon the male and the species."[5] For de Beauvoir, psychoanalysis's diagnosis of clitoral orgasm as "juvenile" is simply an effort to control female sexuality.[6]

The Contemporary Debate

Few of de Beauvoir's contemporaries were interested in female oppression and *The Second Sex* drew on the work of an earlier generation of writers and thinkers. These included Marxist* historians August Bebel* and Friedrich Engels,* who saw the emancipation* of women as key to the success of socialism.* De Beauvoir's work relates these earlier, neglected ideas about women's oppression under capitalism* to the political concerns of her own era.

The only thinker from de Beauvoir's own generation to share her vision was her partner Jean-Paul Sartre.* Like de Beauvoir, Sartre's interest in women's oppression was rooted in a Marxist and existentialist view of social alienation* where class, wealth, race, and religion all play a role in marginalizing certain people. His writings on oppression included *Anti-semite and Jew* (1946) about persecution of Jewish* people, and *Orphée Noire* (1948) about the anti-colonialist* poetry of black intellectuals in the French *négritude** movement.[7]

After World War II,* de Beauvoir was particularly interested in human rights and social equality, as were many on the French political Left. Yet *The Second Sex* was a sharp criticism of the Left's failure to take the emancipation of women as seriously as that of the French colonies and the Jewish people.

De Beauvoir's interest in the nature of female sexuality was shared by the American sexologist* Alfred Kinsey.* But Kinsey was openly critical of *The Second Sex*, arguing it had little to contribute to the public's understanding of sexuality.[8] Kinsey shared a similar public image to de Beauvoir. He too attracted both deep curiosity and outrage from a conservative society that was not used to talking so openly about sex.

Kinsey's books *Sexual Behavior in the Human Male* (1948) and *Sexual Behavior in the Human Female* (1953) received a lot of attention in the United States.[9] Both de Beauvoir and Kinsey were openly criticized for their unorthodox sex lives (Kinsey's involved sleeping with his subjects),[10] and controversy over their private affairs was used to discredit their work. Kinsey having sex with his subjects was seen as an abuse of power. De Beauvoir's acknowledged role in persuading some of her young students to sleep with Sartre was first criticized as improper, and later as a form of subservience that contradicted her feminist* views.[11]

---

1. Simone de Beauvoir, *The Second Sex*, trans. H. M. Parshley (New York: Alfred A. Knopf, 1953), xxix.

2. De Beauvoir, *The Second Sex*, 44.

3. De Beauvoir, *The Second Sex*, 672.

4. De Beauvoir, *The Second Sex*, 71.

5. De Beauvoir, *The Second Sex*, 71, 426.

6. De Beauvoir, *The Second Sex*, 71, 426.

7. Jean-Paul Sartre, *Anti-semite and Jew: An Exploration of the Etiology of Hate*, trans. George Becker (New York: Schocken, 1948); "Orphée Noire," in *Anthologie de la nouvelle poésie nègre et malgache de langue française*, ed. Leopold S. Senghor (Paris: Presse Universitaires de France, 1977).

8. Wardell Poweroy, *Dr Kinsey and the Institute for Sex Research* (New Haven, CT: Yale University Press, 1982), 279.

9. Alfred C. Kinsey et al., *Sexual Behavior in the Human Male* (Bloomington: Indiana University Press, 1975); *Sexual Behavior in the Human Female* (Bloomington: Indiana University Press, 1998).

10. James H. Jones, *Alfred C. Kinsey: A Public/Private Life* (New York: Norton, 1997).

11. Jo-Ann Pilardy, "Feminists Read *The Second Sex*," in *Feminist Interpretations of Simone de Beauvoir*, ed. Margaret A. Simons (University Park: Pennsylvania State University Press, 1995), 40.

THE AUTHOR'S CONTRIBUTION

KEY POINTS

* Simone de Beauvoir's *The Second Sex* addresses women's oppression through the ages.

* Her critique of marriage, analysis of the social and economic factors stacked against women, and revelations about the myths* of femininity helped to fuel the feminist* movement.

* *The Second Sex* highlights how cultural myths about women are deeply rooted in all areas of culture.

Author's Aims

Simone de Beauvoir wrote *The Second Sex* to reveal the full extent of women's oppression and to show how sexist* myths about femininity pervade every corner of society. To do this she divided the book into two parts. Book One was titled *Facts and Myths*, and Book Two was *Women's Life Today*.

Book One examines the history of female subjugation,* or how women have been brought under control. De Beauvoir begins with how different academic disciplines (including biology and psychology*) helped maintain gender stereotypes. The second section shows how women throughout history have been denied "concrete" freedoms, by which she means actual rights such as owning property or taking part in politics. De Beauvoir argues that without concrete freedoms women cannot see themselves as individuals. The belief that women were "inessential" prevented them from claiming the right to concrete freedoms. The end of Book One throws a spotlight on myths about femininity in the work of five authors: Henry de Motherlant,* D. H.

Lawrence,* Paul Claudel,* André Breton,* and Stendhal.* All share the same message:"that woman freely recognizes [Man] as her destiny."[1]

In Book Two, de Beauvoir moves on to the enduring legacy of the ideas discussed in Book One. Each section examines a stage of womanhood (childhood, adolescence, marriage, motherhood) or a cultural female figure (the prostitute, the lesbian, the single woman). De Beauvoir works through these stages and roles, challenging established ideas about each one. So in the chapter on homosexuality, for example, de Beauvoir criticizes the diagnosis of lesbianism as a form of arrested development that manifests itself in women who have not attained full sexual maturity. Some psychologists of the time suggested that lesbianism was merely evidence that a woman had not matured beyond adolescence.[2] De Beauvoir argues instead that lesbianism is, in fact, a rejection of society's expectation that women should marry and have children:"Woman's homosexuality is one attempt among others to reconcile her autonomy* with the passivity of her flesh." Put simply, it is a refusal to be penetrated and conquered by a man and to bear his children.[3]

> "The historical and literary culture to which [the little girl] belongs, the songs and legends with which she is lulled to sleep, are one long exaltation of man. It was men who built up Greece, the Roman Empire, France, and all other nations ... Children's books, mythology, stories, tales, all reflect the myths born of the pride and the desires of men; thus it is that through the eyes of men the little girl discovers the world and reads therein her destiny."
>
> —— Simone de Beauvoir, *The Second Sex*

Approach

De Beauvoir explains that throughout history women have been objects of exchange between fathers and husbands. The father gives his daughter to her husband with a dowry* of money or land, to compensate for the cost of supporting her. The husband takes the bride because she will have his children. Working women earn less than men because it is assumed their income is simply additional to what her husband earns. For these reasons "men have always held the lot of woman in their hands; and they have determined what it should be, not according to her interest, but rather with regard to their own projects, their fears, and their needs."[4]

De Beauvoir also shows how girls are brought up to want to be wives and mothers. Playing with dolls teaches girls to identify with the doll:"the little girl pampers her doll and dresses her as she dreams of being dressed and pampered; inversely, she thinks of herself as a marvelous doll."[5] She learns that "to please she has to be 'pretty as a picture'; she tries to resemble an image."[6] In this way, the little girl develops "the need ... to be admired and to exist for others."[7]

For de Beauvoir, only existentialist* thought can really shed light on these ideas, for it allows women to conceive of themselves in terms other than those that have been imposed on them from their social context. The basic existentialist idea of free will— which says human beings can shape the course of their own lives—provides a way for women to liberate themselves from the constraints and pressures of society at large:"Underlying all individual drama ... there is an existentialist foundation that alone enables us to understand in its unity that particular form of human being which we call a human life."[8]

Women's oppression is rooted in society's view of women not as individuals but as "an existent who is called upon to make herself object."[9] All this can change, though. Since femininity is learned it can also be unlearned. Sexual inequality is not founded on how bodies are different, but on how those differences are explained. Women who challenge the interpretation can take control of their lives. De Beauvoir's existentialist approach offers a way to understand the roots of women's oppression and also a way to overcome it.

Contribution in Context

One of the most original and enduring achievements of *The Second Sex* is the way it challenges long-held cultural myths about women and proves that they are embedded in all areas of culture, from literature and art to psychology. De Beauvoir warns that academics are not immune to these myths because they are also part of wider culture.

She highlights popular myths such as the evil stepmother (who seduces a widower and enslaves his children) and the highly sexed woman (who refuses to settle down with one man) that turn up time and again in Western culture, including in medical assessments and psychiatric profiles. She points out that there is no term for the male equivalent of *nymphomania*, used by doctors to describe excessive sexual desire in women. Such terms reinforce the notion that such sexual desire in a woman is abnormal.

Among de Beauvoir's most original and important insights is that the various expectations of women are incompatible with each other. A woman cannot be sexy seducer, virgin saint, self-sacrificing mother, child-like *ingénue*,* and timid housewife all at the same time. Trying to achieve this impossible task means women cannot cultivate independent or coherent identities of their own.[10]

---

1. Simone de Beauvoir, *The Second Sex*, trans. H. M. Parshley (New York: Alfred A. Knopf, 1953), 172.
2. De Beauvoir, *The Second Sex*, 381.
3. De Beauvoir, *The Second Sex*, 382.
4. De Beauvoir, *The Second Sex*, 119.
5. De Beauvoir, *The Second Sex*, 304.
6. De Beauvoir, *The Second Sex*, 304.
7. De Beauvoir, *The Second Sex*, 304.
8. De Beauvoir, *The Second Sex*, 54.
9. De Beauvoir, *The Second Sex*, 381.
10. De Beauvoir, *The Second Sex*, 185.

SECTION 2
IDEAS

MODULE 5
MAIN IDEAS

KEY POINTS

* Simone de Beauvoir's *The Second Sex* argues that the world has always been run for the benefit of men.

* De Beauvoir insists that women must be treated as equal to men if civilization is to advance.

* She traces the long history of women's secondary status, argues they are effectively treated as objects, and examines what lies behind popular ideas about what it is to be female.

Key Themes

In *The Second Sex*, Simone de Beauvoir looks at the broad sweep of history to chart the oppression of women from earliest times to the modern day. She argues that the world is run for the benefit of men first and women second.

Her challenge to this patriarchal* society has several themes— sexual equality, female objectification* (treating women as objects), socio-economic unfairness, and how cultural myths* influence the way people behave and think.

De Beauvoir sets out to analyze gender relations* in every area of life. She covers the home and the workplace, the social sphere and politics, literature and art, religion and popular culture. She writes about the roots of women's status as secondary citizens, then explores what their oppression means for society as a whole.

The book investigates deep-seated beliefs about femininity, showing how women are taught from childhood to view themselves negatively in relation to men. Her analysis of gender relations shows how women's lives are shaped by the ambitions and desires of their fathers, brothers, and husbands: "To pose woman is to pose the absolute Other,* without reciprocity, denying against all experience that she is a subject, a fellow human being."[1] Traditional institutions such as marriage, de Beauvoir argues, result in women's enslavement by relegating them to the roles of wife, mother, servant, and caretaker.

De Beauvoir's main argument is that these oppressive forces are not only damaging to women, but to society as a whole. She proposes that equality between the sexes is *necessary* for human progress, and that female emancipation* would benefit all society. In *The Second Sex* she champions egalitarianism,* the belief that all humans should be treated the same way. She insists that women and men are not inherently different, but that society treats them as being different.

> "To recognize in woman a human being is not to impoverish man's experience ... To discard the myths is not to destroy all dramatic relation between the sexes ... it is not to do away with poetry, love, adventure, happiness, dreaming. It is simply to ask that behavior, sentiment, passion be founded upon the truth."
>
> —— Simone de Beauvoir, *The Second Sex*

Exploring the Ideas

The Second Sex argues that women have been oppressed since the beginning of the human race. This makes the fight for emancipation (or liberation) twice as difficult because, unlike Jewish* people or African Americans, women have no previous experience of freedom and no shared history.[2]

De Beauvoir shows that women have never held domestic and public influence at the same time. For example, she notes how in Ancient Greece women had legal powers such as the right to buy or sell property but they had virtually no power in the home. The women's quarters were at the back of the house, and mothers had no control over their children's upbringing.[3] Women in Ancient Rome, by contrast, had no legal powers but inhabited the central quarters of the home, and had limited powers such as the right to manage the servants and their children's tutors. For de Beauvoir, these instances show that women's legal freedom comes at the expense of domestic freedom, and domestic freedom comes at the expense of legal freedom. Only men have both.

This means "woman's place in society is that which man assigns to her; at no time has she ever imposed her own law." And since men have greater economic, political, and social power, they also play a more prominent role in cultural and historical events. De Beauvoir observes, "it is not the inferiority of women that has caused their historical insignificance: it is rather their historical insignificance that has doomed them to inferiority."[4]

De Beauvoir argues that this inferior status influences all aspects of a woman's experience. Building on the existentialist* idea that identity is produced rather than being something that is inside of us from the very start, de Beauvoir argues that "one is not born, but rather becomes a woman."[5] In other words, femininity is learned. The criteria for defining femininity also ensure that women see themselves as inferior.

For de Beauvoir, femininity is a social construct* with a political subtext. That means our understanding of feminine behavior is influenced by custom, culture, and language, all designed to underline women's inferior status to men. We associate femininity with physical weakness and emotional vulnerability, reinforcing the belief that women are unsuitable for the workforce or for positions of leadership.

Language and Expression

De Beauvoir saw herself first and foremost as a writer of novels and autobiographies. It may be the reason why her philosophical* writings are much more accessible than those of her contemporaries. Compared with the work of fellow thinker and de Beauvoir's partner Jean-Paul Sartre,* her writing is largely free of jargon. She assumes little knowledge of psychoanalysis* or existentialist thought on the reader's part, and explains tricky theoretical concepts clearly before giving her reasons for opposing them.

For English-language readers, the text's main challenge is how it was abridged. The original French version of *The Second Sex* is more than 900 pages long, but the book's first translator, H. M. Parshley,* cut out nearly 300 pages. He left out significant chunks of two of its most important sections, including the one on history and the essay on marriage.

Philosopher Margaret Simons* argued that Parshley, a

zoologist, was not qualified to translate a book on philosophy and the book suffered as a result. For one thing, Parshley frequently used language that undermined de Beauvoir's arguments. For example, he translated the French word for "humanity", *humanité*, as "mankind."[6] He also mistranslated a number of important philosophical concepts. The existentialist term de Beauvoir and Sartre used to define human consciousness, *etre-pour-soi*—whose standard English translation is "being-for-itself "—implies the potential for free will. Parshley translated it as various versions of "in accordance with one's true nature," distorting its meaning.

Although these issues did not necessarily reduce the work's impact on mainstream audiences (existentialism would, after all, have been quite foreign to them), it did affect the work's critical reception and how it was used by English-speaking philosophers.[7]

For decades, de Beauvoir's English-language publishers Alfred A. Knopf shrugged off requests by French scholars for a new translation, complete with the missing sections. It was only in 2009 that a new English-language version appeared. In 2012 an updated edition of *The Second Sex* was published with previously absent material—including the many biographies of women from history that Parshley left out. However, these new editions were also heavily criticized by de Beauvoir scholar Toril Moi* for allegedly mistranslating the original text.[8] It is important that any reader studying the text in translation is at least aware of these issues.

1. Simone de Beauvoir, *The Second Sex*, trans. H. M. Parshley (New York: Alfred A. Knopf, 1953), 238.

2. De Beauvoir, *The Second Sex,* xviii.

3. De Beauvoir, *The Second Sex*, 124.

4. De Beauvoir, *The Second Sex*, 71.

5. De Beauvoir, *The Second Sex*, 122.

6. Margaret A. Simons, "The Silencing of Simone de Beauvoir: Guess What's Missing from *The Second Sex*," *Women's Studies International Forum* 6, no. 5 (1983): 559–664. See also Margaret A. Simons, "*The Second Sex*: From Marxism to Radical Feminism," in *Feminist Interpretations of Simone de Beauvoir,* ed. Margaret A. Simons (University Park: Pennsylvania State University Press, 1995), 243–62.

7. Simons, "*The Second Sex*."

8. Toril Moi, "The Adulteress Wife," *London Review of Books* 32, no. 11 (February 2010), accessed February 2, 2015, www.lrb.co.uk/v32/n03/toril-moi/the-adulteress-wife.

SECONDARY IDEAS

KEY POINTS

- *The Second Sex* is also an examination of the images of womanhood that appear in all areas of culture, especially those that push the idea that motherhood and sexuality are mutually exclusive.

- De Beauvoir suggests that women who do not conform to society's norms are generally viewed as "wild" and need to be tamed.

- She equates the taking of a woman's virginity with a man's need to assert his power. This line of thought can be traced to issues regarding female genital mutilation* today.

Other Ideas

The Second Sex by Simone de Beauvoir takes a close look at related cultural myths* that underpin our understanding of female sexuality. First among these is the myth of the mother and the whore. De Beauvoir puts the power of this myth down to society's reverence for motherhood—and the attitude that motherhood and sexuality are mutually exclusive.

Throughout history and across cultures, women's main purpose has been seen to be to marry and bear their husbands' children.[1] The mother is revered because she helps the species to continue by having children, while women who reject motherhood are stigmatized or characterized in a negative sense. Promiscuity and infidelity by women undermine the institutions of marriage and motherhood,[2] so these women are labeled whores.[3] "The unwed mother causes scandal and for the child the birth is a stain,"[4] while unfaithful wives have been burned alive or stoned to death.

De Beauvoir points out that society does not hold men to these same standards. "Man, for reasons of prudence, vows his wife to chastity, but he is not himself satisfied with the regime imposed upon her."[5] This is because society recognizes that "marriage kills love" and that husbands are prone to regard their wives "less as a sweetheart than as the mother of their children."[6] Infidelity and prostitution are merely seen as useful means of sexual release for frustrated husbands. The saying that "prostitutes are to the city what sewers are to a palace"[7] conveys the practical function of prostitution. Like the sewers that cleanse a palace, ensuring inhabitants don't end up festering in their own filth, prostitutes allow married men to regularly "expel" their sexual frustrations to keep their marriage intact and society functioning. "The prostitute is a scapegoat; man vents his turpitude upon her."[8]

For de Beauvoir, the mother, the whore, and the prostitute operate in relation to one another to preserve the institution of marriage. "It is in contrast to the sanctified woman that the bad woman stands out in full relief."[9] The myth of the whore is based in the idealization of motherhood. In the same way the "caste of 'shameless women'"—prostitutes—"allows the 'honest woman' to be treated with the most chivalrous respect."[10]

> "One of the most basic problems of woman … is the reconciliation of her reproductive role and her productive labor. The fundamental fact that from the beginning of history doomed woman to domestic work and prevented her taking part in the shaping of the world was her enslavement to the generative function."
>
> ——Simone de Beauvoir, *The Second Sex*

Exploring the Ideas

De Beauvoir also reveals how all of the qualities associated with female emancipation*—strength of character, independent thought, resistance to authority—have been combined in the figure of the wild woman that society wants to domesticate.[11] But society also appreciates that conquest is more enjoyable when the opponent or prey puts up a fight. So the opinionated woman is allowed to voice her ideas not because society wants to hear them, but because it wants to enjoy silencing her. "Man is master of a reality all the more worthy of being mastered in that it is constantly evading control."[12]

De Beauvoir shows how this myth creeps into literature, where a man is often pitted against a spirited female who ends up submitting to his will. She cites William Shakespeare's* *The Taming of the Shrew* (1590–3)* where the male protagonist Petruchio uses psychological* ploys to win over and tame the strong-minded Katerina. In the end, Katerina is tamed into submission and Petruchio "calls his neighbors in to see how authoritatively he can subdue his wife."[13]

Historical figures of female emancipation such as the suffragette* (who fought for the right to vote) and the bluestocking* (a term for female intellectuals) have been similarly viewed as wild animals to be domesticated. De Beauvoir notes that a woman seeking emancipation has to be perceived either as a shrew—a particularly assertive woman—or as a source of sexual attraction. Either way, she risks not being heard for what she is really demanding—liberation.

Overlooked

While de Beauvoir's take on motherhood and sexual desire have been examined extensively, her reading of the myth of virginity has largely been overlooked. This area warrants further study, given its relevance to current discussions about female genital mutilation (FGM). This ritual is practiced in a number of African, Asian, and Middle Eastern countries, as well as among populations in other parts of the world. It is done to control women's sexuality. Clitoridectomy (the amputation of the external part of the clitoris) is designed to prevent female pleasure, while infibulation (the sewing up of the labia) is supposed to preserve a woman's virginity until marriage. This marks her as a closed space to be opened up by her husband. The symbolic meanings attached to FGM cast a new light on *The Second Sex* and its treatment of the virgin.

De Beauvoir equates the act of taking a woman's virginity with power. The virgin is an object of desire the man wishes to have all to himself: "The surest way of asserting that something is mine is to prevent others from using it."[14] Also, as "nothing seems to a man to be more desirable than what has never belonged to any human being," de Beauvoir makes an explicit connection between taking a woman's virginity and the annexing of unoccupied land.[15] These are ways a man "proves" himself through the act of possession.

Taking a woman's virginity allows man to reaffirm himself. "Man fulfills himself as a being by carnally possessing a being."[16] In primitive times, marriage was a form of abduction:"in taking his wife by force [the husband] demonstrates that he is capable of annexing the wealth of strangers and bursting the bounds of destiny."[17] For de Beauvoir, the act of sex is associated with violence and with power. In the same way, FGM is based on the myth of the virgin, enforcing the idea that women are objects of exchange or conquest and that their bodies need to be governed.

1. Simone de Beauvoir, *The Second Sex*, trans. H. M. Parshley (New York: Alfred A. Knopf, 1953), 523.
2. De Beauvoir, *The Second Sex*, 178.
3. De Beauvoir, *The Second Sex*, 177.
4. De Beauvoir, *The Second Sex*, 177.
5. De Beauvoir, *The Second Sex*, 523.
6. De Beauvoir, *The Second Sex*, 524.
7. De Beauvoir, *The Second Sex*, 95.
8. De Beauvoir, *The Second Sex*, 524.
9. De Beauvoir, *The Second Sex*, 179.
10. De Beauvoir, *The Second Sex*, 524.
11. De Beauvoir, *The Second Sex*, 143.
12. De Beauvoir, *The Second Sex*, 164.
13. De Beauvoir, *The Second Sex*, 95.
14. De Beauvoir, *The Second Sex*, 143.
15. De Beauvoir, *The Second Sex*, 143.
16. De Beauvoir, *The Second Sex*, 131.
17. De Beauvoir, *The Second Sex*, 68.

MODULE 7
ACHIEVEMENT

KEY POINTS

* With *The Second Sex*, Simone de Beauvoir succeeded in drawing attention to the inferior social status of women and why they were largely missing from academia, literature, art, and politics.

* The book was truly groundbreaking for its radical views, leading to the Roman Catholic Church* placing it on a list of forbidden books.

* The book can be seen as dated, but this only shows how successfully de Beauvoir's ideas changed society.

Assessing the Argument

Simone de Beauvoir's *The Second Sex* is an unprecedented attack on how society forces women into a subordinate position. The text sheds light on how sexism* is woven throughout human history and it draws attention to the absence of women in academic fields such as philosophy,* psychology,* and history.

Many of de Beauvoir's arguments were entirely new and challenged the conservative values of postwar France. When discussing the low number of female university graduates, de Beauvoir highlights a survey in which the majority of female respondents agreed that "boys are better than girls: they are better workers."[1] De Beauvoir argues that women are brought up to view themselves as less capable than men and this limits their ambitions and chances of success. A working woman considers it "meritorious enough if she earns her own living [for] she could have entrusted her lot to a man."[2]

The book began a radical new discussion around what women could hope to achieve outside of the home. While it would be another 20 years before French women gained either prominence in the workplace, the book's publication was an important step towards the liberation of women from traditional roles.

De Beauvoir was also the first writer to openly challenge society's assumptions about women's sexuality. "It is claimed that woman needs sexual activity less than men: nothing is less certain," she tells us in her chapter on social life.[3] These beliefs, she argues, stem from the fact that "the love act is still considered a *service* woman renders to man, which therefore makes him seem her master."[4] Elsewhere she says that abortion and contraception are a right. Women are entitled to sexual pleasure and should have the freedom to choose if and when to have children.[5] These claims challenged France's deeply ingrained ideas about marriage and sexual relations and anticipated the sexual revolution* by more than a decade.

> "It is not [women's] inferiority that has caused their historical insignificance: it is their historical insignificance that has doomed them to inferiority."
>
> ——Simone de Beauvoir, *The Second Sex*

Achievement in Context

De Beauvoir's work was a significant achievement not only for the rigor of its argument and the strength of its ideas, but for its sheer audacity. The book's explicit content and radical views were completely at odds with the intense conservativism and pronatalism (the championing of having children) of the period.

The Vichy regime* that governed France during World War II* from 1940 to 1944 only reluctantly allowed women to work, and made the distribution of contraceptives a punishable offence.[6] Housewife Marie-Jeanne Latour was executed by guillotine in 1943 for performing abortions.[7] Although women's role in the French Resistance* against the Nazi* occupation gained them the right to the vote, both the Roman Catholic Church and the government continued to stress the importance of motherhood and family. For a woman such as de Beauvoir to discuss female sexuality and to openly question how desirable it was to have children was shocking.

The way de Beauvoir examined gender relations* and her explicit account of the female orgasm—depending not on biology, but on "the whole situation lived by the subject"[8]—were seen as an affront to sexual morality. The fact that she saw the radical sexologist* Alfred Kinsey's* assessment of female masturbation as limited, arguing that it was, in fact, "much more widespread"[9] than even he claimed, shows just how extreme her views were for the time.

The book's explicit content led the Vatican to place it on the Index of Forbidden Books,* where it remains to this day.[10] De Beauvoir also received angry letters from male readers who called her everything from "unsatisfied" and "frigid" to "nymphomaniac" and "lesbian."[11] At the same time, the book clearly had an effect on mainstream society. Interviews conducted decades after publication reveal how many French women read it in secret and were informed by its ideas.[12] In English-speaking countries the response to *The Second Sex* was less hostile. This was partly due to the less prominent role of the Roman Catholic Church, and partly because British and American readers did not view it as a personal attack on their culture, as French readers had.[13]

Limitations

The Second Sex is a product of its time and was published before important events such as the invention of oral contraception, the legalization of abortion in France, the sexual revolution, and the gay rights movement.* It was written when women were a minority of the French workforce and were seldom seen graduating from university. The role of women in society has changed radically since that time and few readers today will find the book as shocking as its first audiences did in 1949.

Yet the fact that de Beauvoir's book has dated can be seen as a clear indication of its success. *The Second Sex* effectively wrote itself into history precisely because it challenged and then changed Western society. Thanks to de Beauvoir's efforts, Western women live in a world that is very different from the one she describes.

The Second Sex has drawn criticism from some French feminists who see it as hostile to women. De Beauvoir was a devotee of egalitarianism,* intent on dismantling socially constructed* differences between people. For her, femininity is a construct and men and women are not different. Biology is not destiny. Second-wave feminists* in France from the 1960s, such as Luce Irigaray,* Hélène Cixous,* Antoinette Fouque,* and Julia Kristeva,* saw de Beauvoir's efforts to ignore gender difference as forcing women to assimilate patriarchal* values and become men.

As this generation of French feminists reclaimed traditional female activities as valid forms of experience, it distanced itself from de Beauvoir. Today de Beauvoir's work is applied less in her home country than in the United States and Britain.[14] After her death in 1986, Fouque suggested that now de Beauvoir was buried, French feminism could forget her "universalist, egalitarian, assimilatory and normalizing feminist positions" and move into the twenty-first century.[15]

---

1. Simone de Beauvoir, *The Second Sex*, trans. H. M. Parshley (New York: Alfred A. Knopf, 1953), 658.

2. De Beauvoir, *The Second Sex*, 658.

3. De Beauvoir, *The Second Sex*, 521.

4. De Beauvoir, *The Second Sex*, 521.

5. De Beauvoir, *The Second Sex*, 464.

6. Toril Moi, *Simone de Beauvoir: The Making of an Intellectual Woman* (New York: Oxford University Press, 1994), 187. See also Francine Muel-Dreyfus, *Vichy et L'Éternel Feminin* (Paris: Editions du Seuil, 1996).

7. Sheila Rowbotham, "Foreword," in Simone de Beauvoir, *The Second Sex*, trans. Candace Borde and Sheila Malovany-Chevalier (New York: Vintage, 2009).

8. De Beauvoir, *The Second Sex*, 71.

9. De Beauvoir, *The Second Sex*, 71.

10. Elizabeth Ladenson, "Censorship," in *The Book: A Global History*, ed. Michael F. Suarez and H. R. Wooudhuysen (Oxford: Oxford University Press: 2013), 173.

11. Sonia Kruks, *Simone de Beauvoir and the Politics of Ambiguity* (Oxford: Oxford University Press, 2012), 48.

12. Catherine Rodgers, "The Influence of *The Second Sex* on the French Feminist Scene," in *Simone de Beauvoir's* The Second Sex: *New Interdisciplinary Essays*, ed. Ruth Evans (Manchester: Manchester University Press, 1998), 67.

13. Margaret A. Simons, "The Silencing of Simone de Beauvoir," *Women's Studies International Forum* 6, no. 5 (1983): 559–664.

14. Moi, *Simone de Beauvoir*, 97–8.

15. Moi, *Simone de Beauvoir*, 97.

PLACE IN THE AUTHOR'S WORK

KEY POINTS

* With the benefit of hindsight, de Beauvoir believed that the views she held in *The Second Sex*, though very radical in 1949, had in fact not been militant enough.

* De Beauvoir suggested her partner Jean-Paul Sartre* first pushed her to examine women's social conditions. Scholars have since questioned this view.

* Despite her many works of fiction and memoir, *The Second Sex* remains de Beauvoir's most famous and well-regarded work.

Positioning

Simone de Beauvoir began work on *The Second Sex* in 1946, three years after the publication of her first novel, *She Came to Stay*. She wrote the book in 14 months while working on another essay titled *The Ethics of Ambiguity*, and published extracts of *The Second Sex* in *Les Temps Modernes*,* the journal she founded with her partner and fellow thinker Jean-Paul Sartre in 1945.

The Second Sex marked a relatively early point in de Beauvoir's career, coming before much of her feminist activism. De Beauvoir did not even declare herself a feminist* until much later, in 1972, when she joined the *Mouvement de libération des femmes* (Women's Liberation Movement).[*1] In an interview with feminist publisher Alice Schwarzer that same year, titled "The Revolutionary Woman," de Beauvoir said that *The Second Sex* had not been militant enough. De Beauvoir had believed socialism* could emancipate* women and there was no need for a feminist struggle. She changed her mind when she saw that socialism had done as little for women as capitalism* had.[2]

In another interview with John Gerassi in 1976, de Beauvoir also said *The Second Sex* was too theoretical and was limited by its focus on the conditions of white, middle-class women and her own personal experiences. What she believed feminism now needed was a book "rooted in practice" and authored by "a whole group of women, from all sorts of countries, and amassed from all classes."[3]

De Beauvoir also revised her view that solidarity among women was difficult to achieve in the face of women's loyalty to their husbands. She did so after witnessing strikes by female factory workers in the 1960s. When their husbands complained, working-class women came together to rebel:"they became committed to a double struggle: the class struggle against the [factory] bosses, the police, the government, etc., on the one hand, and the sex struggle against their own husbands."[4]

> *"I am merely presenting the reality of what happens to women in our society. It is up to my readers to profit from their mistakes, to learn from their experiences and to keep themselves free from situations that end in the same way."*
>
> —— Simone de Beauvoir, cited in Deirdre Bair,
> *Simone de Beauvoir: A Biography*

Integration

In her 1963 autobiography *Force of Circumstance*, de Beauvoir actually recalls a moment of revelation when she understood that "this was a masculine world" and her childhood had been "sustained by myths* invented by men."[5] She suggests it was her partner and fellow existentialist* writer Jean-Paul Sartre who urged her to examine the social condition of women.

Scholars such as Margaret Simons* and Edward and Kate Fullbrook* have recently questioned the truth of this account. De Beauvoir's diaries, published after her death, suggest she had been applying existentialist thought to the condition of women as early as her postgraduate days studying philosophy* at the École Normale Supérieure in Paris.[6] *The Second Sex* can therefore be seen as either the beginning of de Beauvoir's feminism, or her first attempt to articulate her ideas in public.

Either way, the book stands out for its important contribution to existentialist thought and the way it mixes philosophical analysis with autobiographical reflection, always a defining feature of de Beauvoir's work. De Beauvoir never claimed to be unbiased. She used her experiences as a woman to fuel the work with her own anger.[7]

Like *She Came to Stay* (1943), and later *The Mandarins* (1954), *The Second Sex* was addressed to an audience that knew about her unorthodox views on sexuality and her open relationship with Sartre. Her cultivation of this radical image affected the response to *The Second Sex* in both positive and negative ways. It led to intense controversy but also cast her as a heroine and a symbol of sexual freedom.[8] For her supporters, de Beauvoir's open, childless relationship with Sartre proved that women could aspire to something beyond marriage or motherhood.

Significance

The Second Sex is de Beauvoir's best-known work. While her novels and early essays are restricted to the fields of literary criticism* and philosophy, *The Second Sex* has influenced scholarship in fields as diverse as sociology,* history, and political science.* It also informs branches of study such as feminist historical studies and queer theory.*

Within political science, Gill Underwood and Khursheed Wadia have written about de Beauvoir's views on French feminism's difficult relationship with institutional politics, and her efforts, as a member of the *Mouvement de libération des femmes*,* to legalize abortion without resorting to party politics.[9] For these academics, *The Second Sex* offers an important jumping-off point for considering French feminism's history of anti-parliamentarism—that is, the rejection of and effort to overturn political institutions.

The Second Sex also remains an important document for Anglo-American feminist critics, who apply its ideas in the discussion of women's rights,* both in lecture theaters and the wider world. Influential American feminists such as Camille Paglia* and Judith Butler* credit de Beauvoir with having an important influence on their work.[10] De Beauvoir's ideas are to be found in many introductions to feminist thought, especially those on being "made" a woman and the role of reproduction in oppression.

Feminist scholar Frederika Scarth uses de Beauvoir's analysis of women's reproductive role as socially produced to consider how "the enslavement of the species that women experience on a biological level, and in the situation of early nomadic societies, is reproduced illegitimately within patriarchy."*[11] What this means is that women's biological role as mothers is used to restrict them within specific arenas such as the home, and to deny other aspects of their identity. Scarth uses de Beauvoir's ideas to discuss the politics of motherhood. More recently, in *Women in Philosophy: What Needs to Change?* (2013), Karina Hutchison and Fiona Jenkins* identify *The Second Sex* as the first attempt to ask why women were left out of philosophical debate. They argue that the situation has not changed:"the exclusion of women, or, put differently, the fostering of men" in the discipline remains a pressing concern.[12] De Beauvoir's work remains relevant to these contemporary debates.

1. Claire Laubier, *The Condition of Women in France: 1945 to the Present—A Documentary Anthology* (London: Routledge, 1992), 19.

2. Alice Schwarzer, *After the Second Sex: Conversations with Simone de Beauvoir* (London: Pantheon, 1984).

3. John Gerassi, "Interview with Simone de Beauvoir: *The Second Sex*, 25 Years Later," *Society* (January-February 1976), accessed May 5, 2015, www.marxists.org/reference/subject/ethics/de-beauvoir/1976/interview.htm.

4. Gerassi, "Interview with Simone de Beauvoir."

5. Jean Leighton, *Simone de Beauvoir and Women* (Madison, NJ: Farleigh Dickinson University Press, 1975), 24.

6. Nancy Bauer, "Must We Read de Beauvoir?" in *The Legacy of Simone de Beauvoir*, ed. Emily Grosholz (New York: Oxford University Press, 2004), 125.

7. De Beauvoir, "Interview."

8. *Daughters of de Beauvoir*. Film produced by Penny Foster, 1988.

9. Gill Underwood and Khursheed Wadia, *Women and Politics in France: 1958–2000* (London and New York: Routledge, 2000), 156.

10. Camille Paglia, *Sex, Art, and American Culture: Essays* (New York: Penguin Books); Judith Butler, *Gender Trouble: Feminism and the Subversion of Identity* (London: Routledge, 1990).

11. Fredrika Scarth, *The Other Within: Ethics, Politics and the Body in Simone de Beauvoir* (New York: Rowman & Littlefield, 2004), 141–2.

12. Karina Hutchison and Fiona Jenkins, *Women in Philosophy: What Needs to Change?* (Oxford: Oxford University Press, 2013), 9.

SECTION 3
IMPACT

THE FIRST RESPONSES

KEY POINTS

* When *The Second Sex* appeared in 1949 many critics attacked the book as an outrageous insult to the sexual morals of the day.

* De Beauvoir was openly ridiculed and insulted in France, but English-speaking readers were more receptive to her ideas.

* There has been a lot of fierce debate about exactly how much influence *The Second Sex* had on the French feminists* who came after de Beauvoir.

Criticism

French society after World War II* was deeply conservative. Simone de Beauvoir's direct challenge to social and sexual propriety in *The Second Sex* sparked such fury that Roman Catholic* novelist François Mauriac* used it as the basis for a campaign against decadence in literature.[1] An article in a conservative newspaper called the book a "disgusting apology for sexual inversion and abortion."[2]

The French political Left dismissed the book as a work of bourgeois* (middle-class) decadence. It was criticized for "exalting the lowest in man: bestial instincts, sexual depravity"[3] and left-wing philosopher Albert Camus* said it made French men look ridiculous.[4] However, according to de Beauvoir's friend, the anthropologist* Claude Levi-Strauss,* this was because "A *woman* existentialist* was more than [the establishment] could bear." [5]

This generally negative view of the text has endured in France, as critics have argued that de Beauvoir's own role, in soliciting and seducing younger women for Jean-Paul Sartre, undermined her feminist principles.[6] She stands accused of failing to recognize the disrespectful treatment of both herself and other women by her lover, the philosopher Sartre, since in seducing these women and passing them on to Sartre, she made herself a tool for Sartre's pleasure, and an accessory to their exploitation. She also stands accused of exploiting younger women, since the student she seduced in 1939 was underage, and of trying to abolish laws on the age of sexual consent.[7] Jean-Raymond Audet described *The Second Sex* as a work of profound "narcissism."*[8] Intellectual interest in *The Second Sex* in France today is rare, with the notable exception of feminist philosopher Michèle Le Doeuff.* In *Hipparchia's Choice* (1990) she examines *The Second Sex* in the context of de Beauvoir's difficult relationship with philosophy* and in relation to Sartre's well-documented contempt for women.[9]

The Second Sex had a warmer reception in Britain and America. Of the 20 books on de Beauvoir published between 1980 and 1992, 17 were in English.[10] The first English-language study of her work, Elaine Marks's* *Simone de Beauvoir: Encounters with Death* in 1973, also introduced *The Second Sex* to a wider readership.

These scholars suggest that French criticism of de Beauvoir often reads as a thinly veiled dislike of women. The Norwegian American feminist writer Toril Moi* notes, "The implication is that whatever a woman says, or writes, or thinks is less important than what she *is.*"[11] So painting de Beauvoir as a narcissist or as Sartre's slave effectively depoliticizes her, reducing *The Second Sex* to the rants of an overemotional woman.[12]

> *"In actuality the relation of the two sexes is not quite like that of two electrical poles, for man represents both the positive and the neutral, as is indicated by the common use of* man *to designate human beings in general, whereas woman represents only the negative, defined by limiting criteria, without reciprocity."*
>
> —— Simone de Beauvoir, *The Second Sex*

Responses

Soon after *The Second Sex* appeared, de Beauvoir stopped going out to avoid being harassed in the street by angry readers.[13] She was not too surprised. Her publisher rejected an earlier collection of short stories because of its explicit sexual content. She also lived through the outcry against her first novel, 1943's *She Came to Stay*, a fictionalized account of her and Sartre's affair with two of de Beauvoir's female students.[14]

Yet this uproar made *The Second Sex* famous, winning de Beauvoir attention from publishers in the United States and public-speaking roles at home and abroad over many years. The most noteworthy was a 1975 televised interview, "Why I am a Feminist," where she returned to her central theme: "Being a woman is not a natural fact. It's the result of a certain history. There is no biological or psychological* destiny that defines a woman as such ... Baby girls are manufactured to become women."[15]

The Second Sex was first published in 1949. In 1972 she publically abandoned the belief that a socialist revolution* would bring sexual equality and declared herself a feminist. This revised outlook informed the activism of her later years. She said any follow-up to *The Second Sex* needed multiple authors and a practical approach. Feminism "must derive [its] theory from practice, not the other way around" and must reflect the needs of all classes and cultures.[16] De Beauvoir never gave up on egalitarianism,* though, and was suspicious of differential feminism*, the idea that men and women are equal but also different. For de Beauvoir "it falls again into the masculine trap of wanting to enclose us in our differences."[17]

Conflict and Consensus

Fierce debate surrounds the importance or otherwise of de Beauvoir's ideas, but *The Second Sex* had a clear impact on mainstream readers. Thousands of French women were influenced by reading the book in secret before the 1970s,[18] while the public view of *The Second Sex* shifted in line with the radical movements and civil unrest of the 1960s. French factory workers demanded better conditions, ethnic minorities fought institutional racism,* and in 1968 the women's rights movement* was born.

This is where the arguments start. Toril Moi has written extensively on French feminism's disregard for *The Second Sex*. She interprets this as springing from a rejection of existentialist thought that casts de Beauvoir as a "theoretical dinosaur."[19]

Catherine Rodgers,* however, says Moi does not acknowledge de Beauvoir's influence on French egalitarian feminists, and even de Beauvoir failed to recognize her own legacy.[20] Rodgers argues that leaders of the *Mouvement de libération des femmes** would certainly have read *The Second Sex*. She puts the book's absence from feminist writings of the era down to the fact that its arguments had become commonplace.[21]

De Beauvoir claimed that second-wave feminists* in France (1960s to late 1980s) "may have become feminists for the reasons that I explain in *The Second Sex*, but they discovered those reasons in their life experiences, not in my book." [22] Scholars continue to debate whether she is right.

---

1. Ursula Tidd, *Simone de Beauvoir* (London: Routledge, 2004), 101.

2. As cited in Sylvie Chaperon, *Les années Beauvoir: 1945–1970 (The Beauvoir Years: 1945–1970)* (Paris: Fayard, 2000), 182; and Margaret A. Simons, "Introduction," in *Simone de Beauvoir: Feminist Writings*, ed. Margaret A. Simons and Marybeth Timmermann (Chicago: University of Illinois Press, 2015), 4–5.

3. As cited in Chaperon, *Les années Beauvoir,* 175–7.

4. Tidd, *Simone de Beauvoir*, 101.

5. Simone de Beauvoir, *Lettres à Sartre (Letters to Sartre)*, ed. Sylvie le Bon (Paris: Gallimard, 1990), Vol. II, 284, as cited in Margaret A. Simons, "*The Second Sex*: From Marxism to Radical Feminism," in *Feminist Interpretations of Simone de Beauvoir*, ed. Margaret A. Simons (University Park: Pennsylvania State University Press, 1995), 2.

6. Toril Moi, *Simone de Beauvoir: The Making of an Intellectual Woman* (New York: Oxford University Press, 1994), 98.

7. Eric Berkowitz, *Sex and Punishment: Four Thousand Years of Judging Desire* (Berkeley, CA: Counterpoint, 2012).

8. Jean-Raymond Audet, *Simone de Beauvoir face à la morte* (Lausanne: Éditions L'Age de L'Homme, 1979), 122–5.

9. Michèle Le Doeuff, *Hipparchia's Choice*, trans. Trista Selous (New York: Columbia University Press, 1990).

10. Moi, *Simone de Beauvoir*, 96.

11. Moi, *Simone de Beauvoir*, 98.

12. Moi, *Simone de Beauvoir*, 101.

13. Tidd, *Simone de Beauvoir*, 102.

14. Tidd, *Simone de Beauvoir*, 102.

15. Jean-Louis Servan-Schreiber, "Why I Am a Feminist: Interview with Simone de Beauvoir [1975]," accessed March 5, 2015, www.youtube.com/ watch?v=v2LkME3MMNk.

16. John Gerassi, "Interview with Simone de Beauvoir: *The Second Sex*, 25 Years Later," *Society* (January-February 1976), accessed May 5, 2015, www.marxists.org/reference/subject/ethics/de-beauvoir/1976/interview.htm.

17. Margaret A. Simons and Jessica Benjamin, "Beauvoir Interview (1979)," in *Beauvoir and the Second Sex*, ed. Margaret A. Simons (New York: Rowman & Littlefield), 19.

18. Catherine Rodgers, "The Influence of *The Second Sex* on the French Feminist Scene," in *Simone de Beauvoir's* The Second Sex: *New Interdisciplinary* Essays, ed. Ruth Evans (Manchester: Manchester University Press, 1998), 64.

19. Moi, *Simone de Beauvoir*, 98.

20. Rodgers, "The Influence of *The Second Sex*," 67.

21. Rodgers, "The Influence of *The Second Sex*," 64.

22. Gerassi, "Interview with Simone de Beauvoir."

THE EVOLVING DEBATE

KEY POINTS

- There have been many different views as to what de Beauvoir meant when defining gender.
- De Beauvoir's work helped to create room in academic scholarship for women's studies* and gender studies.*
- People read *The Second Sex* today to gain insight into a number of different things, from gender and identity to how socio-economic regimes can affect oppression.

Uses and Problems

Simone de Beauvoir's *The Second Sex* remains controversial, not least because it opens up whole new areas of enquiry. Elisabeth Spelman argues that de Beauvoir's work is undermined by concentrating on the oppression of white, middle-class women.[1] Judith Okely,* on the other hand, does not see this as a problem. She says this limited focus offers an opportunity to examine de Beauvoir as a case study, because her work provides insight into the lives of an entire generation of such women in France.

Scholars are also at odds over how useful and accurate de Beauvoir's definition of gender as a social construct* really is. Sociology,* psychology,* and gender studies have all accepted her assertion that identity cannot simply be reduced to anatomy, to the body we are born in. Yet academics have tended to read *The Second Sex* as explicitly denying there is any actual difference between the genders.

Debra Bergoffen* and Moira Gatens have challenged this approach.[2] Both argue that de Beauvoir's understanding of the relationship between the concepts of "feminine," "woman," and "female" is more complicated than just sex versus gender. This suggests de Beauvoir is far more radical than critics understand.[3] Such new readings continue to shed fresh light on *The Second Sex* as part of contemporary gender studies.

> "*Feminine voices are silent when it comes to concrete action ... the true control of the world has never been in the hands of women; they have not brought their influence to bear upon technique or economy, they have not made and unmade states, they have not discovered new worlds. Through them certain events have been set off, but the women have been pretexts rather than agents.*"
>
> —— Simone de Beauvoir, *The Second Sex*

Schools of Thought

The Second Sex is integral to feminism* because it pioneered the public discussion of female sexuality. As Elizabeth Badinter* puts it, de Beauvoir's "message ... was heard by my whole generation."[4]

In the United States and Canada, de Beauvoir inspired the creation of centers for women's studies from the 1970s onwards.[5] Her ideas also played an important role in the sociology of gender, which emerged in the mid-1950s to address how masculinity and femininity are perceived and whether gender is a result of our anatomy or whether it is imposed by our upbringing. The 1970s saw the development of feminist approaches to the sociology of gender, which increasingly used de Beauvoir's argument that gender is a product of culture. In the 1990s gender studies emerged to tackle the perception of gender across culture, including literature, film, and visual art. Gender theorists explore the effects of socialization* on gender and their work is heavily indebted to de Beauvoir.

Within the traditional male-dominated field of philosophy* Janna Thompson* and Dorothy E. Smith* used de Beauvoir's existentialist* feminism to introduce a female perspective. Thompson's edited collection of essays *Women and Philosophy* (1976) explores how philosophy might aid women's emancipation.* She investigates concepts such as individualism, identity, androgyny (the combination of feminine and masculine characteristics), and free will. The essays ask how much a woman's identity is limited by patriarchal* values and whether (in contrast to de Beauvoir's assertion) it can develop independently.[6]

Smith's book, *The Everyday World as Problematic: A Feminist Sociology* (1987), explores the difficulties in developing a feminist sociology. The question "What is a woman?" reminds us that humankind is viewed in male terms. So in the same way, the question "What is feminist sociology?" reminds us that this field is shaped by male interests and views.[7] *The Everyday World as Problematic* marked an important step in challenging feminist scholarship, warning how feminism might end up marginalizing women further.

In Current Scholarship

The Second Sex continues to be read by different people for different reasons. Gender theorists such as Judith Butler* and Moira Gatens see de Beauvoir's work as part of a wider debate about whether gender is inborn or imposed, and whether a woman can forge her own identity despite her condition as "Other."*

Feminist historians and Marxist* thinkers read the book primarily for insights into the role of different socio-economic regimes (particularly capitalism*) in female oppression. For Mary Spongberg's* *Writing Women's History since the Renaissance* (2002), de Beauvoir's ideas are the key to explaining women's perceived absence from history.[8]

The Second Sex is often referenced in introductions to feminist theory, both as a milestone in feminist thought and as an important female perspective on the human sciences. Andrea Nye's* *Feminist Theory and the Philosophies of Man* (2013) pays tribute to the enduring relevance of de Beauvoir's ideas as patriarchal values continue to overshadow philosophical thought and literary interpretations.[9]

Philosophers have an abiding interest in how writer and philosopher Jean-Paul Sartre* influenced de Beauvoir's work. At first it was assumed *The Second Sex* had been shaped by his ideas, leading some to challenge its originality or even to label it self-contradictory. How could a feminist base her work on a philosophy so steeped in Sartre's well-documented misogyny?*[10] But Bergoffen and Christine Daigle* use de Beauvoir's diaries to prove that her ideas pre-dated her relationship with Sartre. It was actually de Beauvoir who influenced *his* work.[11] This debate resulted in *Sartre and Beauvoir: Questions of Influence* (2009), a collection of essays by leading de Beauvoir scholars. They considered how assumptions about Sartre's influence might well have affected the critical reception of *The Second Sex*.[12]

1. Elisabeth Spelman, *Inessential Woman: Problems of Exclusion in Feminist Thought* (Boston: Beacon Press, 1988), 63–4.

2. Debra Bergoffen, "(Re)counting the Sexual Difference," and Moira Gatens, "De Beauvoir and Biology: A Second Look," in *The Cambridge Companion to Simone de Beauvoir,* ed. Claudia Card (Cambridge: Cambridge University Press, 2003), 248–65 and 266–85, respectively.

3. Gatens, "De Beauvoir and Biology," 267; Bergoffen, "(Re)counting the Sexual Difference," 250.

4. Catherine Rodgers, "The Influence of *The Second Sex* on the French Feminist Scene," in *Simone de Beauvoir's* The Second Sex: *New Interdisciplinary* Essays, ed. Ruth Evans (Manchester: Manchester University Press, 1998), 67.

5. Lisa Appignanesi, *Simone de Beauvoir* (London: Haus, 2005), 160.

6. Janna Thompson, *Women and Philosophy* (Bundoora: Australasian Association of Philosophy, 1986).

7. Dorothy E. Smith, *The Everyday World as Problematic: A Feminist Sociology* (Boston: Northeastern University Press, 1987).

8. Mary Spongberg, *Writing Women's History since the Renaissance* (New York: Palgrave Macmillan, 2002).

9. Andrea Nye, *Feminist Theory and the Philosophies of Man* (London: Routledge, 2013).

10. Margery Collins and Christine Pierce, "Holes and Slime: Sexism in Sartre's Psychoanalysis," in *Women and Philosophy*, ed. Carol C. Gould and Marx W. Wartofsky (New York: Capricorn Books, 1976).

11. Margaret A. Simons, "Is *The Second Sex* Beauvoir's Application of Sartrean Existentialism?" paper given at the Twentieth World Congress of Philosophy, Boston, MA, August 10–15, 1998; Edward Fullbrook and Kate Fullbrook, *Sex and Philosophy: Re-thinking de Beauvoir and Sartre* (London: Bloomsbury, 2008).

12. Christine Daigle and Jacob Golomb, eds, *Sartre and Beauvoir: The Question of Influence*, (Bloomington: Indiana University Press, 2009).

MODULE 11
IMPACT AND INFLUENCE TODAY

KEY POINTS

* Many contemporary feminists* argue that modern society's attitudes to women have not changed all that much since de Beauvoir wrote *The Second Sex.*

* Issues of gender and how modern life still wants to construct ideas of what a woman is from a very early age remain topics that arouse passionate feelings on both sides.

* Questions still remain about whether English translations of *The Second Sex* have clouded de Beauvoir's original arguments.

Position

It is difficult to imagine a branch of feminist thought that is not influenced by Simone de Beauvoir's *The Second Sex* as either an inspiration or a source of argument. Feminism has evolved considerably since the book appeared in 1949, but many claims made by contemporary feminists are rooted in its ideas.

Natasha Walter's* *Living Dolls: The Return of Sexism* (2010) takes its title from de Beauvoir's description of women as "marvelous doll[s]."[1] Walter uses *The Second Sex* to argue that Western society has actually changed very little since de Beauvoir's day. She examines developments over the last half-century to show that the effects of post-1960 second-wave feminism were short-lived. Female emancipation* has become synonymous with the right to dress seductively and have casual sex rather than gaining an equal footing in the workplace or politics. Walter echoes the fears de Beauvoir expressed in *The Second Sex*, that it is all too easy for feminism to be folded back into a patriarchal* narrative.[2] So when members of the Russian feminist group Pussy Riot* go topless to protest as a shock tactic, they are actually playing into the male gaze. Pussy Riot's message goes unheard as onlookers focus instead on their breasts.

De Beauvoir's ideas also informed the seminal 1990 work by Judith Butler,* *Gender Trouble.*[3] Butler wants to know how gender identity and sexuality are defined and agrees with de Beauvoir that gender is not biological, but is imposed by culture and society. However, where de Beauvoir argues that patriarchal society views women as a lack or an absence, Butler argues there is no such thing as gender in the first place. Even the distinction between male and female genitalia is false because our understanding is based on social norms. This is to say that our understanding of the difference between male and female genitalia and their connotations is, itself, socially constructed. Butler's controversial text develops de Beauvoir's ideas in important new ways, making us reconsider our understanding of biology and gender.

> *"It was the social regime founded on private property that entailed the guardianship of the married woman, and it is the technological evolution accomplished by men that has emancipated the women of today."*
>
> —— Simone de Beauvoir, *The Second Sex*

Interaction

De Beauvoir's work remains relevant to the public debate, from how girls are told to wear pink to sexism* in the online gaming world. Campaigns to challenge gender bias in children's clothes and toys, for example, include Pinkstinks. Their campaign highlights how toys primarily emphasizing appearance, fashion, and shopping have a damaging effect, severely limiting girls' aspirations. These ideas chime with Peggy Orenstein's and Rebecca Hains's respective books, *Cinderella Ate My Daughter* (2011) and *The Princess Problem* (2014), which tackle how the market divides into "for boys" and "for girls" to increase profits at the expense of children.[4]

Like de Beauvoir, contemporary feminists often face intense criticism. The founders of Pinkstinks receive hate mail from around the world. Laura Bates's* Everyday Sexism Twitter campaign (http://everydaysexism.com/) invites women to share their experiences of sexual discrimination. She was slated by men's rights groups, who argued that the project exaggerated the extent of sexism in society. In 2014, critics of misogyny* (dislike or hatred of women) in the video games industry received hundreds of death threats in a vitriolic campaign that made global headlines."Gamergate" reflected ongoing issues about how women are represented in popular culture. Meanwhile, Caroline Criado-Perez's* 2014 campaign for a woman to appear on UK banknotes resulted in Jane Austen being selected for the £10 note—but also in Criado-Perez receiving death threats on Twitter.

These intense reactions suggest that attitudes to gender identity and sexuality cause feeling to run every bit as high today as when *The Second Sex* first appeared. They show that the project de Beauvoir began is not yet finished. If anything, the anonymity afforded by social media has ushered in a new set of challenges for feminist activists campaigning in the digital arena. The potential for online harassment, stalking, and abuse risks turning the Internet into one further space in which women's actions are curtailed, and their views silenced.

The Continuing Debate

The Second Sex is central to the academic disciplines of gender studies,* queer studies, and feminist criticism. For contemporary scholars, *The Second Sex* remains interesting for its historical, global impact. The work was again in the spotlight in 1983 when the feminist critic Margaret A. Simons* published an important essay, "The Silencing of Simone de Beauvoir." Simons laid out in minute detail the discrepancies between the original French text and the English translation by H. M. Parshley.* He left out between a tenth and a third of the text and was a zoologist with no background in either philosophy* or history. Simons argued that Parshley was not qualified for the job and mistranslated several of the book's central philosophical concepts. He effectively undermined de Beauvoir's feminist argument by translating it into male-oriented terms. For instance, he translated "humanité" as "mankind" rather than "humankind," and "le soi" as "man" rather than "self."

Simons' revelations led some scholars to question whether previous assessments of the book based on Parshley's translation could even be trusted.[5] A new English translation was published in 2009 and an extended version followed in 2012, but again these raised new questions. Feminist writer Toril Moi,* who argued that the true meaning of de Beauvoir's existentialist* argument is skewed by the book's first translation, was appalled by the new version. She claimed it suffered many errors of omission, syntax, and mistranslation.[6]

---

1. Simone de Beauvoir, *The Second Sex*, trans. H. M. Parshley (New York: Alfred A. Knopf, 1953), 304.

2. Natasha Walter, *Living Dolls: The Return of Sexism* (London: Virago, 2010), 129.

3. Judith Butler, "Sex and Gender in Simone de Beauvoir's *Second Sex*," *Yale French Studies* 72 (1986): 35–49, and *Gender Trouble: Feminism and the Subversion of Identity* (London: Routledge, 1990), 11, 13, 190.

4. Peggy Orenstein, *Cinderella Ate My Daughter: Dispatches from the Front Lines of the New Girlie-Girl Culture* (New York: Harper, 2011); Rebecca Hains, *The Princess Problem: Guiding Our Girls through the Princess-obsessed Years* (Naperville, IL: Sourcebooks, 2014).

5. Margaret A. Simons, "The Silencing of Simone de Beauvoir," *Women's Studies International Forum* 6, no. 5 (1983): 559–664.

6. Toril Moi, "The Adulteress Wife," *London Review of Books* 32, no. 3 (February 11, 2010), accessed February 2, 2015, www.lrb.co.uk/v32/n03/ toril-moi/the-adulteress-wife.

WHERE NEXT?

KEY POINTS

- Simone de Beauvoir's *The Second Sex* is still inspiring people to think and write about gender, identity, and feminism* today.
- People are applying de Beauvoir's ideas to interesting new areas, including political science.*
- The impact of *The Second Sex* on modern society and its attitude to women is both huge and undeniable.

Potential

Simone de Beauvoir's claim in *The Second Sex* that "one is not born, but rather becomes a woman"[1] was a rallying cry for feminist activists in the 1970s. Today it is still a powerful idea in discussions about the origins of gender identity and sexual orientation. Some of de Beauvoir's ideas that were radical at the time—that women should be able to work or choose not to have children—are now accepted in Western culture. Likewise, she has been proved right by the discrediting of psychoanalytic* concepts such as "penis envy,"* by both psychologists* and feminist theorists, who have found little basis for it. Indeed, the theory itself has led many feminists to distance themselves from psychoanalysis as a whole, seeing the theory as representative of the discipline's deep-rooted misogyny.*

However, *The Second Sex* still has a lot to offer contemporary discussions about gender and sexuality. *The Second Sex* may prove more useful to twenty-first-century feminists than those in the 1970s and 1980s. The emergence of queer theory* and gender studies* brings new attention to de Beauvoir because they also question the ways we define gender and sexual orientation. Her central argument that femininity is a tool of ideological oppression and that womanhood itself is a social construct* has gained new relevance.

Mariam Motamedi-Fraser's* *Identity Without Selfhood: Simone de Beauvoir and Bisexuality* (1999) is one example of how de Beauvoir's theories are part of contemporary discussions about gender.[2] Motamedi-Fraser examines biographical, media, and academic accounts of de Beauvoir to show the impact of Western ideas about identity and sexuality on scholarly interpretations of her work. Motamedi-Fraser suggests that de Beauvoir's sexual relationships and her writing on sexuality are more complex and subtle than scholars have assumed. The book considers how cultural understandings of sexual orientation in turn shape and inform scholarship—and can lead to misinterpretation.

Toril Moi's* *Simone de Beauvoir: The Making of an Intellectual Woman* (1993) and *What Is a Woman?* (1999) examine de Beauvoir's views on femininity in relation to the whole feminist movement and show how competing theories obscured de Beauvoir's ideas for decades.[3] Margaret A. Simons's* book-length study *Beauvoir and the Second Sex: Feminism, Race and the Origins of Existentialism* (1999) opened up the discussion on links between feminism, anti-colonialism,* and human rights activism.[4] There is potential for more applications of de Beauvoir's work in discussions about women's rights* in the developing world. Echoing de Beauvoir's assertion that patriarchal* societies view women as "not-men," Sharmon Lynette Monogan writes compellingly about the role that patriarchal values play in the tradition of female genital mutilation.*5

> "The period in which we live is a period in transition; this world, which has always belonged to the men, is still in their hands: the institutions and the values of the patriarchal civilization still survive in large part."
>
> —— Simone de Beauvoir, *The Second Sex*

Future Directions

Elizabeth Fallaize,* Toril Moi, and Margaret Simons are de Beauvoir's most vocal champions and their work examines her impact within the history of feminist thought and also within the existentialist* tradition. They have been joined more recently by Ruth Evans,* Eleanor Holveck, Ursula Tidd, Sonia Kruks, and Emily Grosholz, who have all helped to increase de Beauvoir's visibility in the humanities and social sciences.

Holveck's *Simone de Beauvoir's Philosophy of Lived Experience* (2002) examines de Beauvoir's existentialist thought across her fiction and philosophy.* The book takes a fresh approach to *The Second Sex* by relating it to the philosophical essays de Beauvoir wrote earlier in her career.[6] Tidd's *Simone de Beauvoir* (2004) provides fresh readings of all of de Beauvoir's works.[7] Grosholz's *The Legacy of Simone de Beauvoir* (2006) addresses the influence of de Beauvoir on later feminist thought.[8] Kruks's

Simone de Beauvoir and the Politics of Ambiguity (2012) applies her work to the field of political science—a little-explored area that Kruks finds fruitful in discussing women's role in politics.[9] Each of these texts is testament to the enduring relevance of de Beauvoir's book and the scope for new interpretations in light of the cultural shifts that followed.

Summary

The Second Sex is an important investigation into women's oppression throughout history, and a pivotal moment in the emancipation* of women. De Beauvoir shows us exactly how sexism* has seeped into modern society and how it evolved throughout the ages to ensure that women remain submissive. Through her explanation and investigation of popular ideas about femininity, as well as her analysis of women's social and economic dependence on men, de Beauvoir paved the way for the second wave of feminism during the sexual revolution* of the 1960s and into the 1970s. Her work is also used today in discussions about gender identity and sexual orientation.

A twenty-first-century reader might view de Beauvoir's ideas as old fashioned or obvious. But even if some of de Beauvoir's calls to action seem dated (that women should work, for example), the work itself remains intensely relevant. Her analysis remains powerful for its examination of the impact of cultural myths,* the effect of ideas about femininity on child development, and her challenge to traditional definitions of gender and sexuality.

And of course, *The Second Sex* stands out for its historical importance. This is the book that launched the women's rights movement in France. De Beauvoir helped bring about the sexual revolution and feminism as we know it today. As Elizabeth Badinter* commented in her epitaph to de Beauvoir, "Women, you owe everything to her!"[10]

1. Simone de Beauvoir, *The Second Sex*, trans. H. M. Parshley (New York: Alfred A. Knopf, 1953), 249.

2. Mariam Motamedi-Fraser, *Identity Without Selfhood: Simone de Beauvoir and Bisexuality* (Cambridge: Cambridge University Press, 1999).

3. Toril Moi, *Simone de Beauvoir: The Making of an Intellectual Woman* (Oxford and New York: Oxford University Press, 1993); *What Is a Woman?* (Oxford and New York: Oxford University Press, 1999).

4. Margaret A. Simons, *Beauvoir and the Second Sex: Feminism, Race and the Origins of Existentialism* (Lanham, MD, and Oxford: Rowman & Littlefield, 1999).

5. Sharmon Lynette Monogan, "Patriarchy: Perpetuating the Practice of Female Genital Mutilation," *International Research Journal of Arts & Humanities* 37 (2010): 83–99.

6. Eleanore Holveck, *Simone de Beauvoir's Philosophy of Lived Experience* (New York: Rowman & Littlefield, 2002).

7. Ursula Tidd, *Simone de Beauvoir* (London: Routledge, 2004).

8. Emily Grosholz, *The Legacy of Simone de Beauvoir* (Oxford: Oxford University Press, 2006).

9. Sonia Kruks, *Simone de Beauvoir and the Politics of Ambiguity* (Oxford: Oxford University Press, 2012).

10. As cited in Deirdre Bair, *Simone de Beauvoir: A Biography* (London: Cape, 1991), 617.

GLOSSARY OF TERMS

1. **Alienation:** an individual's estrangement from his or her community. It is often referred to in relation to Karl Marx's theory of social alienation, which argued that alienation is a consequence of the unequal distribution of wealth and power.

2. **American Civil Rights movement:** a movement in the United States to secure equal rights for black people, extending to outlawing segregation and removing current discriminatory legislation against blacks. The movement gained sway in the mid-1950s but was at its most intense in the 1960s.

3. **Anthropology:** the study of humans and human behavior, and their cultures. The field draws on a number of others disciplines in the physical, biological, social, and human sciences.

4. **Anti-colonialism:** the critique of or opposition to the system of colonialism and colonial rule, either by the colonized or by external parties who view the system as socially or economical unjust.

5. **Anti-Semitism:** prejudice against, fear of, and discrimination against Jewish people based on their ethnicity, beliefs, and/or heritage.

6. **Autonomy:** the independence and freedom of either action or belief. An autonomous individual is one who can believe and act as s/he wishes.

7. **Bluestocking:** a term used to describe an educated, intellectual woman. It originated in the eighteenth century, but acquired negative connotations in the following century, becoming a term for a frumpy or unattractive bookish woman.

8. **Bourgeois:** a term used in Marxist theory to refer to the wealthy class, which owns the means of production (for example, the owner of a shop, a factory, or any other entity that produces goods or services).

9. **Capitalism:** a mode of production and an economic system in which industries, trade, and the means of production are either largely or entirely privately owned, and in which production and trade are done for profit.

10. **Colonialism:** the rule of one country by another, involving unequal power relations between the rulers (colonists) and ruled (colonies), and the exploitation of the colonies' resources to strengthen the economy of the colonizers' home countries.

11. **Dehumanization:** the systematic process of demonizing another person or persons by making them appear less than human, and therefore not deserving of humane treatment.

12. **Differential feminism:** a strand of feminism that argues the need to recognize that men and women are different, and that seeks to celebrate the different attributes that women offer. For differential feminists, gender equality should not be based on the assumption that women behave like men.

13. **Dowry:** the goods, cash, or property that a bride's family gives to the bridegroom in exchange for agreeing to support her and any children they may have.

14. **Egalitarianism:** the championing of equal treatment, based on the assumption that all humans are equal in worth and social status.

15. **Emancipation:** the procurement of social, economic, and/or political rights or equality by a previously disenfranchised group.

16. **Existentialism/existential humanism:** a branch of philosophy that places emphasis on the human subject's struggle for self-understanding, self-knowledge, and responsibility in the absence of a god.

17. **Female genital mutilation (FGM):** the ritual cutting or removal of some or all of the external female genitalia, which is designed to control women's sexuality by either denying them sexual pleasure, or preserving their virginity before marriage.

18. **Feminism:** a series of ideologies and movements concerned with equal social, political, cultural, and economic rights for women, including equal rights in the home, workplace, education, and government.

19. **French Resistance:** a term used to describe those who opposed the Vichy regime that collaborated with the Nazis in occupied France during World War II. Members of the Resistance published an underground newspaper, provided first-hand intelligence to the Allies, and participated in guerrilla welfare.

20. **Gay rights movement:** refers to a series of events, including public protests, lobbying, and demonstrations from the 1970s to the present day, through which homosexual men and women sought to redress the stigma of homosexuality

and attain equal rights to heterosexuals, including the right to marry and to have children.

21. **Gender relations:** any interaction between the two genders based on the social roles designated to each one.

22. **Gender studies:** the interdisciplinary academic study of gender relations, gender identity, and sexual orientation, including how gender and sexual orientation are perceived and/or represented in culture.

23. **Hegelian dialectics:** a form of philosophical discussion that involves putting forth one's argument (thesis), providing the counterargument (antithesis), and then reaching a conclusion (synthesis) that seeks to reconcile the two.

24. **Historical materialism:** an approach to historical criticism developed by Karl Marx, which examines history in relation to class relations and income inequality.

25. **Index of Forbidden Books:** a list of books banned by the Roman Catholic Church due to allegedly improper content, often regarding sexuality or social behavior that goes against the dictates of the Church.

26. *Ingénue*: a French word for innocent, often used to describe a sheltered, naïve, or sexually inexperienced female.

27. **Interdisciplinarity:** the study of a problem, question, or topic that combines different disciplines, schools of thought, or theoretical approaches.

28. **Jewish:** an ethno-cultural and ethno-religious group that originated in the Ancient Middle East from the Israelites.

29. **Lacanian psychoanalysis:** a branch of psychoanalysis founded by Jacques Lacan that examines the development of identity from early childhood.

30. **Literary criticism:** the evaluation, study, and interpretation of literature.

31. **Malagasy Uprising (1947–8):** a nationalist rebellion against French rule in the French colony of Madagascar. The uprising was violently repressed by the French military, which carried our mass executions, torture, and war rape of the country's inhabitants.

32. **Marxism:** refers to cultural, philosophical, socio-economic, political, and

aesthetic readings based on the work of the nineteenth-century political economist Karl Marx. Marxist theorists and writers are concerned with the growth of social inequality under capitalism, and the influence this has on culture and society.

33. **Matrilineal descent or matrilineality:** a form of hereditary succession that sees the individual as a descendant of his/her mother's family. This pattern contrasts with the more common pattern of patrilineage, which traces descent through the father's family.

34. **Misogyny:** the dislike or hatred of women, and behavior that reflects that hatred, including sexual discrimination against women, violence, denigration, and the treatment of women as passive objects (also known as objectification).

35. *Mouvement de libération des femmes* **(Women's Liberation Movement):** the first women's rights movement in France, founded in 1968, which sought to attain the right to contraception, abortion, and equal rights in the workplace.

36. **Myth or cultural myth:** beliefs born out of a culture's ideology, faith, or world-view.

37. **Narcissism:** excessive self-absorption or interest in one's own self.

38. **Nazis:** also known as the National Socialist Party, they ruled in Germany from 1933 to the end of World War II in 1945, a period known as the Third Reich. Nazi ideology was essentially fascist, and incorporated anti-Semitism and scientific racism.

39. *Négritude:* a literary movement running from the 1930s to the late 1950s, begun by Afro-Caribbean writers living in Paris to protest against French colonial rule and French cultural assimilation.

40. **Objectification:** a philosophical term that refers to any instance in which a person is treated as a thing. The term "female objectification" is commonly used in discussions on gender to refer to the treatment of women as objects without agency or purpose other than attracting, or being attractive to, men.

41. **Obsolescence:** an object, idea, or person's passage into disuse or irrelevance due to the passing of time.

42. **Other:** the term philosophers use for that which is separate or distinct from the

human self.

43. **Patriarchy or patriarchal society:** refers to any social system in which men hold the most power, often in roles of political leadership, are granted privilege in the control of property, hold moral authority, or are granted authority over female relatives and children.

44. **Penis envy:** a term used by psychoanalysts until the mid-1950s. According to this theory, females' transition from childhood to adulthood involves the realization that men have penises and that they do not.

45. **Philosophy:** a field of the humanities that studies fundamental human problems related to reality, knowledge, existence, reason, language, and values.

46. **Political science:** a field of the social sciences that examines government policies and politics, and the dynamics of nation, government, and state.

47. **Proletarian:** in Marxist theory, this is the term used to define the working class, which earns money by working for the bourgeoisie.

48. **Psychoanalysis:** a discipline founded by the Austrian physician Sigmund Freud, which explores the unconscious workings of the human mind and considers the role of repression and desire in human development.

49. **Psychology:** an academic and applied discipline concerning the study and treatment of mental behavior and mental functions.

50. **Queer theory:** an approach to critical theory that questions or rejects traditional ideas of sexuality or gender identity in literary and cultural subjects.

51. **Racism:** refers to both discrimination and prejudice based on the perception of biological differences between people, including race and ethnicity.

52. **Roman Catholic Church:** the largest Christian Church, and among the oldest religious institutions in the world. Its doctrines include the outlawing of abortion and any contraception beyond natural family planning.

53. **Second-wave feminism:** refers to the women's rights movement from the 1960s, coinciding with the sexual revolution and lasting up until the late 1980s. In contrast to first-wave feminism, women at this time were fighting for sexual

emancipation, the legalization of abortion, and equal pay in the workplace.

54. **Sexism:** discrimination or prejudice based on a person's gender. This might include treating a person as an inferior, or making assumptions about them due to their gender.

55. **Sexology:** the study of human sexuality, including sexual interests, functions, and behavior.

56. **Sexual revolution:** a systematic dismantling of traditional social codes and mores regarding sexuality and sexual propriety that took place throughout the United States and Europe from 1960 to 1980. This included the normalization of premarital sex and of the use of contraception, and the legalization of abortion in many countries.

57. **Social construct:** any category or definition used by society to group people together or define them. Social constructs are often used to privilege a particular group over others, for instance men over women, or one race over another.

58. **Socialist revolution:** refers to the overthrow of capitalism and the introduction of a socialist government, which would effect structural changes in society, including the redistribution of wealth and the eradication of social inequality.

59. **Socialization:** the processes by which human beings learn from others, including but not limited to how they absorb systems of belief, learn particular modes of behavior, and develop views about gender, race, or sexuality.

60. **Sociology:** the academic study of social behavior. The discipline examines the origins and development of social relations, their different modes of organization, and different social institutions.

61. **Soviet Union:** a single-party Marxist-Leninist state comprising 15 socialist republics in Eastern Europe, including Russia, Georgia, and the Ukraine, that existed between 1922 and 1991.

62. **Subjugation:** conquering and gaining control of someone or something and rendering them subordinate.

63. **Suffragette:** a term used to describe women in the late nineteenth and early twentieth centuries who fought for the right to vote.

64. ***The Taming of the Shrew* (1590–3):** a play by William Shakespeare, which describes a man's systematic domestication of a rebellious, strong-minded woman (the "shrew" of the title).

65. ***Les Temps Modernes*:** a left-wing journal founded by Jean-Paul Sartre and Simone de Beauvoir in 1945, named after Charlie Chaplin's film *Modern Times.*

66. **Vichy regime (1940–4):** a provisional government installed in France during World War II after France surrendered to Nazi Germany, and which collaborated with the Nazis.

67. ***Women and Socialism*:** a written history of female oppression from prehistoric times to the end of the nineteenth century. Its author, the German socialist August Bebel, argued that women's emancipation was key to the success of socialism.

68. **Women's rights movement:** a series of efforts to attain rights for women equal to those of men. The movement occurred in stages, and rights were gained at different times in different countries. However, it is generally recognized as having reached its height in the late 1960s and early 1970s.

69. **Women's studies:** the interdisciplinary study of gender, sexuality, class, race, and nationhood, which addresses female identity as a combination of these factors. The discipline emerged in the United States in the 1970s and was strongly influenced by second-wave feminism.

70. **World War II (1939–45):** a war fought between Britain, France, the Soviet Union, the United States, and others against Germany, Italy, and Japan.

PEOPLE MENTIONED IN THE TEXT

1. **Elizabeth Badinter (b. 1944)** is a French historian, writer, and professor of philosophy at Paris's École Polytechnique. She is known for her feminist writings, which include the controversial *Conflict, Women, Motherhood* (2010).

2. **Johann Bachoffen (1815–87)** was a German anthropologist and writer best known for his argument that prehistoric and early modern societies were matriarchal—that is, they gave more power to women.

3. **Laura Bates** is a British feminist activist and journalist best known for her Everyday Sexism campaign, which seeks to raise awareness of the sexism women experience on a daily basis.

4. **August Bebel (1840–1913)** was a German socialist writer and politician. He is best known for his book *Women and Socialism* (1879).

5. **Debra Bergoffen** is the Bishop Hamilton Lecturer in Philosophy at American University and Professor Emerita of Philosophy at George Mason University. She writes on contemporary philosophical thought, feminist theory, and human rights.

6. **André Breton (1896–1966)** was a French writer, poet, and visual artist, and one of the founders of Surrealism, a radical artistic movement in the early twentieth century. He is perhaps best known for his novels *Nadja* (1928) and *Mad Love* (1937).

7. **Judith Butler (b. 1956)** is a feminist and scholar of queer theory and gender relations best known for her book *Gender Trouble* (1990), in which she argues that gender is purely a social construct entirely separate from biological or anatomical facts.

8. **Albert Camus (1913–60)** was a French novelist, playwright, existentialist philosopher, and journalist, and was awarded the Nobel Prize for Literature in 1957.

9. **Hélène Cixous (b. 1937)** is a French feminist poet, philosopher, and literary critic, best known for her feminist book *The Laugh of the Medusa* (1975), which urges female readers to escape the phallocentrism (penis-centered nature) of modern language and adopt what she calls "female writing" (écriture féminine).

10. **Paul Claudel (1868–1955)** was a French poet and playwright whose work de Beauvoir criticizes intensely in *The Second Sex* for its misogynistic depiction of women.

11. **Caroline Criado-Perez (b. 1984)** is an English journalist and feminist activist known for her efforts to allow women better representation in the British media, and to be depicted on banknotes. This last campaign resulted in the Bank of England's decision to put Jane Austen on the £10 banknote by 2017.

12. **Christine Daigle** is professor of philosophy at Brock University in California, specializing in existentialism, phenomenology, and feminist theory in the continental tradition.

13. **Friedrich Engels (1820–95)** was a German philosopher and close colleague of Karl Marx, with whom he wrote *The Communist Manifesto* (1848). His book *The Origins of the Family, Private Property and the State* (1884) inspired many of de Beauvoir's ideas, and is now considered an important text by feminist scholars.

14. **Ruth Evans** is Dorothy McBride Orthwein Professor at Saint Louis University in Missouri, specializing in Middle English literature (1300–1580) and feminist theory and criticism.

15. **Elizabeth Fallaize (1950–2009)** was a British academic, feminist, leading figure in French studies, and international authority on the work of Simone de Beauvoir, including both her novels and philosophical writings.

16. **Antoinette Fouque (1936–2014)** was a French psychoanalyst and feminist activist who co-founded France's women's rights movement, the *Mouvement de libération des femmes*, in 1968. She is recognized as one of the country's most pre-eminent feminists.

17. **Kate Fullbrook (1951–2003)** was an American-born academic best known for campaigning in the UK for the right to a liberal education, and for her writings on feminist theory, modernist fiction by women, and Simone de Beauvoir's relationship with Sartre.

18. **Georg Wilhem Friedrich Hegel (1770–1831)** was a German philosopher

and a major figure in the Idealism movement. He became well known for his historicist and realist accounts of reality. His concept of a "system" of integration between mind and nature, subject and object, and so on, was one of the first conceptual moves that acknowledged contradictions and oppositions within such a system.

19. **Luce Irigaray (b. 1930)** is a Belgian-born French feminist philosopher, linguist, and cultural theorist best known for *Speculum of the Other Woman* (1974) and *This Sex Which Is Not One* (1977).

20. **Fiona Jenkins** is a senior lecturer in the School of Philosophy at the Australian National University, specializing in contemporary French philosophy.

21. **Alfred Kinsey (1894–1956)** was an American biologist and professor of zoology best remembered for his pioneering work in the field of sexology, which he recounted in the books *Sexual Behavior in the Human Male* (1948) and *Sexual Behavior in the Human Female* (1953).

22. **Julia Kristeva (b. 1941)** is a Bulgarian French feminist philosopher, psychoanalyst, and literary critic best known for her books *Powers of Horror* (1982), *Woman's Time* (1981), and *Black Sun* (1992).

23. **Jacques Lacan (1901–81)** was a French psychoanalyst and psychiatrist best known for his development of Lacanian psychoanalysis, which had a profound influence on French philosophy and feminist theory.

24. **D. H. Lawrence (1885–1930)** was a British novelist, short-story writer, and essayist best known for his novel *Lady Chatterley's Lover* (1928), whose explicit sexual content resulted in it being censored for many years.

25. **Michèle Le Doeuff (b. 1948)** is a French philosopher and feminist writer, best known for *Hipparchia's Choice: An Essay Concerning Women, Philosophy, Etc.* (1991) and *The Sex of Knowing* (1998).

26. **Claude Lévi-Strauss (1908–2009)** was a French ethnologist and anthropologist, and is frequently cited as the "father of modern anthropology."

27. **Elaine Marks (1930–2001)** was a leading authority on French literature, feminist theory, and women's writing, and is best remembered for her

groundbreaking books on Simone de Beauvoir and Colette.

28. **Karl Marx (1818–83)** was a German political philosopher and economist whose analysis of class relations under capitalism and articulation of a more egalitarian system provided the basis for communism.

29. **François Mauriac (1885–1970)** was a French novelist and a laureate of the 1952 Nobel Prize in Literature, who has, however, been criticized for promoting misogynistic views in his novels.

30. **Toril Moi (b. 1953)** is a Norwegian-born American feminist writer and de Beauvoir scholar who has written prolifically on de Beauvoir's role in the feminist movement in France and the United States, including *Sexual/Textual Politics* (1985), *Simone de Beauvoir: The Making of an Intellectual Woman* (1994), and *What Is a Woman? And Other Essays* (1999).

31. **Lewis Henry Morgan (1818–81)** was an American anthropologist and social theorist. He is best remembered for his claim that the earliest domestic institution (family) was based on matrilineal lines. Members were identified by their mother's lineage, and descent was traced through the mother's family.

32. **Mariam Motamedi-Fraser** is reader of sociology at Goldsmiths (University of London), and is best known for her writings on Islam and the Middle East, feminist theory, and sexuality.

33. **Henry de Motherlant (1895–1972)** was a French writer renowned for his misogynistic views, exemplified in his series of four anti-feminist novels, *Les Jeunes Filles (The Young Girls)*. De Beauvoir devoted an entire chapter of *The Second Sex* to a discussion of his anti-feminist stance.

34. **Andrea Nye (b. 1939)** is a feminist writer and philosopher best known for her writings on feminist philosophy, including *Words of Power: A Feminist Reading of the History of Logic* (1990) and *Feminism and Modern Philosophy: An Introduction* (2004).

35. **Judith Okely (b. 1941)** is Emeritus Professor of Sociology and Anthropology at the University of Hull. She is best known for her writings on Simone de Beauvoir, as well as her work on identity, autobiography, and anthropological practice.

36. **Camille Paglia (b. 1947)** is an American social critic, academic, and "dissident" feminist best known for her harsh criticism of feminist academia and women's studies, her controversial stance on many feminist issues, and her veneration of Simone de Beauvoir.

37. **H. M. Parshley (1884–1953)** was the first translator of *The Second Sex*. His English translation has been criticized for cutting out substantial portions of the original, and for often translating terms such as "human" as "man" and "humankind" as "mankind," perpetuating the male-centrism de Beauvoir's book was critiquing.

38. **Pussy Riot:** a Russian feminist punk-rock group that protests against the oppression of women, as well the leadership of their government.

39. **Catherine Rodgers** is associate professor of languages, translation, and communication at Swansea University in Wales. She writes on contemporary French women's writing, feminist theory, Marguerite Duras, and Simone de Beauvoir.

40. **Jean-Paul Sartre (1905–80)** was a leading French existential philosopher, and de Beauvoir's lifetime partner and colleague. His work relied heavily on the idea that individuals are "condemned to be free," and that there is no creator.

41. **William Shakespeare** (1564–1616) was an English playwright, actor, and poet, and regarded as one of the most eminent English-language writers to have ever lived. His plays include *Romeo and Juliet*, *Hamlet*, *Macbeth*, *Othello*, and *King Lear* as well as *The Taming of the Shrew*.

42. **Margaret A. Simons** is an American feminist philosopher and critic who has written widely on de Beauvoir and feminist criticism as a whole.

43. **Dorothy E. Smith (b. 1926)** is a Canadian sociologist, feminist, and women's studies theorist, and one of the founders of the sociological sub-disciplines of feminist standpoint theory (which traces authority back to individuals' knowledge) and institutional ethnography (which maps individuals' relations within social institutions such as the workplace).

44. **Mary Spongberg** is an Australian academic specializing in feminist theory,

modern history, and women's history, and the editor of the international journal *Australian Feminist Studies*. She is also the author of *Feminizing Venereal Disease* (1995).

45. **Joseph Stalin** (1878–1953) was one of the leaders of the Russian Revolution in 1917, and the leader of the Soviet Union from the mid-1920s until his death in 1953.

46. **Stendhal (1783–1842)** was the pen name of Marie-Henri Beyle, a nineteenth-century French writer, best remembered for his novels *The Charterhouse of Parma* (1839) and *The Red and the Black* (1830).

47. **Janna Thompson** is professor of philosophy at La Trobe University in Australia. She writes on political philosophy, human rights, feminist theory, and ethics.

48. **Natasha Walter (b. 1967)** is a feminist writer and activist best known for her books *The New Feminism* (1998) and *Living Dolls: The Return of Sexism* (2010).

49. **Naomi Wolf (b. 1962)** is a contemporary feminist critic, journalist, and writer best known for leading what she retrospectively called third-wave feminism, and for her book *The Beauty Myth* (1991).

50. **Mary Wollstonecraft (1759–97)** was an English philosopher, writer, and advocate of women's rights, best known for *A Vindication of the Rights of Woman* (1792), in which she championed women's right to an education.

51. **Virginia Woolf (1882–1941)** was an English novelist and essayist known for her innovative, experimental writing style and her radical views on women. She is best known for novels such as *Mrs Dalloway* (1925) and *Orlando* (1928), and for her feminist essay *A Room of One's Own* (1929).

 **WORKS CITED**

1. Appignanesi, Lisa. *Simone de Beauvoir*. London: Haus, 2005.

2. Audet, Jean-Raymond. *Simone de Beauvoir face à la morte*. Lausanne: Éditions L'Age de L'Homme, 1979.

3. Bair, Deirdre. *Simone de Beauvoir: A Biography*. London: Cape, 1991. Bates, Laura. *Everyday Sexism*. London: Simon & Schuster, 2014.

4. Bauer, Nancy. "Must We Read de Beauvoir?" In *The Legacy of Simone de Beauvoir*, edited by Emily Grosholz. New York: Oxford University Press, 2004.

5. Beauvoir, Simone de. *Pyrrhus et Cinnin*. Paris: Gallimard, 1944.

6. *The Second Sex*. Translated by H. M. Parshley. New York: Vintage, 1953.

7. *She Came to Stay*. Translated by Roger Senhouse and Yvonne Moyse. New York: W. W. Norton & Co.,1954 (English translation of *L'Invitée*. Paris: Gallimard, 1943).

8. *Lettres à Sartre* (*Letters to Sartre*). Edited by Sylvie le Bon. Paris: Gallimard, 1990.

9. *The Mandarins*. Translated by Leonard M. Friedman. New York: W. W. Norton & Co., 1991 (English translation of *Les mandarins*. Paris: Gallimard, 1954).

10. *The Ethics of Ambiguity*. Translated by Bernard Frechtman. New York: Citadel Press, 1996 (English translation of *Pour une morale de l'ambiguité*. Paris: Gallimard, 1947).

11. Bebel, August. *Women and Socialism*. Translated by Meta L. Stern. New York: Socialist Literature Company and Co-operative Press, 1910.

12. Bergoffen, Debra. "(Re)counting the Sexual Difference." In *The Cambridge Companion to Simone de Beauvoir,* edited by Claudia Card, 248–65. Cambridge: Cambridge University Press, 2003.

13. Berkowitz, Eric. *Sex and Punishment: Four Thousand Years of Judging Desire*. Berkeley, CA: Counterpoint, 2012.

14. Butler, Judith. "Sex and Gender in Simone de Beauvoir's Second Sex." *Yale French Studies* 72 (1986): 35–49.

15. *Gender Trouble: Feminism and the Subversion of Identity*. London: Routledge, 1990.

16. Chaperon, Sylvie. *Les années Beauvoir: 1945–1970 (The Beauvoir Years: 1945–1970)*. Paris: Fayard, 2000.

17. Daigle, Christine, and Jacob Golomb, eds. *Sartre and Beauvoir: The Question of Influence*. Bloomington, IN: Indiana University Press, 2009.

18. Evans, Alfred B. *Soviet Marxism-Leninism: The Decline of an Ideology*. Westport, CT: Praeger, 1993.

19. Evans, Ruth, ed. *Simone de Beauvoir's* The Second Sex*: New Interdisciplinary Essays*. Manchester: Manchester University Press, 1998.

20. Fallaize, Elizabeth, ed. *Simone de Beauvoir: A Critical Reader*. New York: Routledge, 1998.

21. Fullbrook, Edward, and Kate Fullbrook. *Sex and Philosophy: Re-thinking de Beauvoir and Sartre*. London: Bloomsbury, 2008.

22. Gatens, Moira. "De Beauvoir and Biology: A Second Look." In *The Cambridge Companion to Simone de Beauvoir,* edited by Claudia Card, 266–85.

23. Cambridge: Cambridge University Press, 2003.

24. Gerassi, John. "Interview with Simone de Beauvoir: *The Second Sex*, 25 Years Later." *Society*, January-February (1976). Accessed May 5, 2015. www.marxists.org/reference/subject/ethics/de-beauvoir/1976/interview.htm.

25. Grosholz, Emily. *The Legacy of Simone de Beauvoir*. Oxford: Oxford University Press, 2006.

26. Hains, Rebecca. *The Princess Problem: Guiding Our Girls through the Princess-obsessed Years*. Naperville, IL: Sourcebooks, 2014.

27. Holveck, Eleanore. *Simone de Beauvoir's Philosophy of Lived Experience*. New York: Rowman & Littlefield, 2002.

28. Hutchison, Karina, and Fiona Jenkins. *Women in Philosophy: What Needs to Change?* Oxford: Oxford University Press, 2013.

29. Jones, James H. *Alfred C. Kinsey: A Public/Private Life.* New York: Norton, 1997.

30. Kelly-Gadol, Joan. "The Social Relation of the Sexes: Methodological Implications of Women's History." In *Feminism and Methodology: Social Science Issues,* edited by Sandra G. Harding. Bloomington and Indianapolis, IN: Indiana University Press, 1987.

31. Kinsey, Alfred C., Wardell B. Pomeroy, and Paul H. Gebhard. *Sexual Behavior in the Human Male.* Bloomington, IN: Indiana University Press, 1975.

32. *Sexual Behavior in the Human Female.* Bloomington, IN: Indiana University Press, 1998.

33. Kruks, Sonia. *Simone de Beauvoir and the Politics of Ambiguity.* Oxford: Oxford University Press, 2012.

34. Ladenson, Elizabeth. "Censorship." In *The Book: A Global History*, edited by Michael F. Suarez and H. R. Wooudhuysen, 164–82. Oxford: Oxford University Press, 2013.

35. Laubier, Claire. *The Condition of Women in France: 1945 to the Present-A Documentary Anthology.* London: Routledge, 1992.

36. Le Doeuff, Michèle *Hipparchia's Choice.* Translated by Trista Selous. New York: Columbia University Press, 1990.

37. Leighton, Jean. *Simone de Beauvoir and Women.* Madison, NJ: Farleigh Dickinson University Press, 1975.

38. Moi, Toril. *Simone de Beauvoir: The Making of an Intellectual Woman.* New York: Oxford University Press, 1994.

39. *What Is a Woman?* Oxford and New York: Oxford University Press, 1999.

40. *Sexual/Textual Politics.* London and New York: Routledge, 2002.

41. "The Adulteress Wife." *London Review of Books* 32, no. 3. (February 11, 2010). Accessed February 2, 2015. www.lrb.co.uk/v32/n03/toril-moi/the-adulteress-wife.

42. Monogan, Sharmon Lynette. "Patriarchy: Perpetuating the Practice of Female

Genital Mutilation." *International Research Journal of Arts & Humanities* 37 (2010): 83–99.

43. Motamedi-Fraser, Mariam. *Identity Without Selfhood: Simone de Beauvoir and Sexuality.* Cambridge: Cambridge Cultural Social Studies, 1999.

44. Muel-Dreyfus, Francine. *Vichy et L'Éternel Feminin.* Paris: Editions du Seuil, 1996.

45. Nye, Andrea. *Feminist Theory and the Philosophies of Man.* London: Routledge, 2013.

46. Orenstein, Peggy. *Cinderella Ate My Daughter: Dispatches from the Front Lines of the New Girlie-Girl Culture.* New York: Harper, 2011.

47. Paglia, Camille. *Sex, Art and American Culture: Essays.* New York: Penguin Books, 1992.

48. Pilardy, Jo-Ann. "Feminists Read *The Second Sex.*" In *Feminist Interpretations of Simone de Beauvoir,* edited by Margaret A. Simons. University Park, PA: Pennsylvania State University Press, 1995.

49. Poweroy, Wardell. *Dr Kinsey and the Institute for Sex Research.* New Haven, CT: Yale University Press, 1982.

50. Rodgers, Catherine. "The Influence of *The Second Sex* on the French Feminist Scene." In *Simone de Beauvoir's* The Second Sex: *New Interdisciplinary Essays,* edited by Ruth Evans. Manchester: Manchester University Press, 1998.

51. Rowbotham, Sheila. "Foreword." In Simone de Beauvoir, *The Second Sex,* translated by Candace Borde and Sheila Malovany-Chevalier. New York: Vintage, 2009.

52. Sartre, Jean-Paul. *Anti-semite and Jew: An Exploration of the Etiology of Hate.* Translated by George Becker. New York: Schocken, 1948 (English translation of *Réflexions sur la question juive.* Paris: Éditions Morihien, 1944).

53. "Orphée Noire." In *Anthologie de la Nouvelle poésie nègre et malgache de langue francaise,* edited by Leopold S. Senghor. Paris: Presse Universitaires de France, 1977.

54. "Existentialism and Humanism." In *Jean-Paul Sartre: Basic Writings*, edited by Stephen Priest, 20–57. New York: Routledge, 2002.

55. Scarth, Fredrika. *The Other Within: Ethics, Politics and the Body in Simone de Beauvoir*. New York: Rowman & Littlefield, 2004.

56. Schwarzer, Alice. "The Revolutionary Woman." In *After the Second Sex: Conversations with Simone de* Beauvoir. London: Pantheon, 1984.

57. Servan-Schreiber, Jean-Louis. "Why I Am a Feminist: Interview with Simone de Beauvoir [1975]." Accessed March 5, 2015. www.youtube.com/watch?v=v2LkME3MMNk.

58. Simons, Margaret A. "The Silencing of Simone de Beauvoir: Guess What's Missing from *The Second Sex*." *Women's Studies International Forum* 6, no. 5 (1983): 559–664.

59. "*The Second Sex*: From Marxism to Radical Feminism." In *Feminist Interpretations of Simone de Beauvoir,* edited by Margaret A. Simons, 243–62. University Park, PA: Pennsylvania State University Press, 1995.

60. "Is *The Second Sex* Beauvoir's Application of Sartrean Existentialism?" Paper given at the Twentieth World Congress of Philosophy, Boston, MA, August 10–15, 1998.

61. *Beauvoir and the Second Sex: Feminism, Race and the Origins of Existentialism*. Oxford: Rowman & Littlefield, 1999.

62. ed. *Feminist Interpretations of Simone de Beauvoir*. University Park, PA: Pennsylvania State University Press, 1995.

63. Simons, Margaret A., and Jessica Benjamin. "Beauvoir Interview (1979)." In *Beauvoir and the Second Sex*, edited by Margaret A. Simons, 1–22. New York: Rowman & Littlefield, 2001.

64. Smith, Dorothy E. *The Everyday World as Problematic: A Feminist Sociology*. Boston: Northeastern University Press, 1987.

65. Spelman, Elisabeth. *Inessential Woman: Problems of Exclusion in Feminist Thought.* Boston: Beacon Press, 1988.

66. Spongberg, Mary. *Writing Women's History since the Renaissance*. New York: Palgrave Macmillan, 2002.

67. Thompson, Janna. *Women and Philosophy*. Bundoora: Australasian Association of Philosophy, 1986.

68. Tidd, Ursula. *Simone de Beauvoir*. London: Routledge, 2004.

69. Underwood, Gill, and Khursheed Wadia. *Women and Politics in France: 1958–2000*. London and New York: Routledge, 2000.

70. Walter, Natasha. *Living Dolls: The Return of Sexism*. London: Virago, 2010.

71. Woolf, Virginia. *A Room of One's Own*. London and New York: Penguin, 2002.

原书作者简介

西蒙娜·德·波伏娃生于 1908 年，是一位才华横溢的学者。她激进的观点和备受非议的爱情生活令法国和世界震惊。她处于 20 世纪存在主义思潮（以个人的选择取代上帝的哲学）的最前沿。直至 1986 年去世，她始终是一位多产且引人注目的哲学家、小说家和自传作家。她最重要的著作《第二性》提出了"身为女人意味着什么"的问题，推动了 20 世纪西方女权运动的开展。

本书作者简介

拉凯莱·迪尼博士曾就读于剑桥大学、伦敦国王学院和伦敦大学学院。她目前的许多著作关注现当代英美小说中对生产和消费的呈现。她曾在剑桥大学国际教育基金会任教。目前，她在罗汉普顿大学任英语讲师。她的第一部专著《20 世纪小说中的消费主义、废物与再利用：先锋派的遗产》于 2016 年由英国帕尔格雷夫麦克米伦出版社出版。

世界名著中的批判性思维

《世界思想宝库钥匙丛书》致力于深入浅出地阐释全世界著名思想家的观点，不论是谁、在何处都能了解到，从而推进批判性思维发展。

《世界思想宝库钥匙丛书》与世界顶尖大学的一流学者合作，为一系列学科中最有影响的著作推出新的分析文本，介绍其观点和影响。在这一不断扩展的系列中，每种选入的著作都代表了历经时间考验的思想典范。通过为这些著作提供必要背景、揭示原作者的学术渊源以及说明这些著作所产生的影响，本系列图书希望让读者以新视角看待这些划时代的经典之作。读者应学会思考、运用并挑战这些著作中的观点，而不是简单接受它们。

ABOUT THE AUTHOR OF THE ORIGINAL WORK

Born in Paris in 1908, **Simone de Beauvoir** was a gifted scholar whose radical ideas and scandalous love life shocked France and the wider world. She was at the forefront of twentieth-century existentialism—the philosophy that replaced God with personal choice. De Beauvoir was a prolific and high profile writer of philosophy, fiction, and autobiography until her death in 1986. *The Second Sex*, her essential book about what it means to be a woman, inspired the feminist movement.

ABOUT THE AUTHOR OF THE ANALYSIS

Dr Rachele Dini studied at Cambridge, King's College London and University College London. Much of her current work focuses on the representation of production and consumption in modern and contemporary Anglo-American fiction. She has taught at Cambridge and for the Foundation for International Education, and is now Lecturer in English at the University of Roehampton. Her first monograph, *Consumerism, Waste and Re-use in Twentieth-century Fiction: Legacies of the Avant-Garde*, was published by Palgrave Macmillan in 2016.

ABOUT MACAT
GREAT WORKS FOR CRITICAL THINKING

Macat is focused on making the ideas of the world's great thinkers accessible and comprehensible to everybody, everywhere, in ways that promote the development of enhanced critical thinking skills.

It works with leading academics from the world's top universities to produce new analyses that focus on the ideas and the impact of the most influential works ever written across a wide variety of academic disciplines. Each of the works that sit at the heart of its growing library is an enduring example of great thinking. But by setting them in context — and looking at the influences that shaped their authors, as well as the responses they provoked — Macat encourages readers to look at these classics and game-changers with fresh eyes. Readers learn to think, engage and challenge their ideas, rather than simply accepting them.

批判性思维与《第二性》

首要批判性思维技巧：分析

次要批判性思维技巧：理性化思维

西蒙娜·德·波伏娃于 1949 年出版的《第二性》是一部女权主义批评和哲学杰作。这本书对战后女性在法国社会中的地位进行了煽动性的描述，它有助于定义 20 世纪后半叶女权主义思潮的主要趋势，时至今日，它的影响力犹存。

此书的成功在很大程度上归功于德·波伏娃出色的写作风格和写作激情，但二者都来源于她清晰的批判性思维技巧。她构建了强有力的论据来反驳那些无声的假设，这些假设曾不断（且仍然）贬低女性的地位，使其在这个由男性支配的社会中处于"次要地位"。德·波伏娃还展示了她出色的核心推理技能：举出有说服力的案例，组织好观点，用论据来支撑结论。

不过最重要的是，《第二性》在分析水平上堪称大师级作品。由于德·波伏娃把当代的社会和文化结构作为一系列论据，认为这些结构持续具有贬低女性的倾向，所以她能够看清并描述巩固男性支配地位的隐含假设。她对这些假设的解构为她提供了关键的信息去论证女性绝非"第二"性，她们与男人在各方面都是平等的。

CRITICAL THINKING AND *THE SECOND SEX*

- Primary critical thinking skill: ANALYSIS
- Secondary critical thinking skill: REASONING

Simone de Beauvoir's 1949 book *The Second Sex* is a masterpiece of feminist criticism and philosophy. An incendiary take on the place of women in post-war French society, it helped define major trends in feminist thought for the rest of the 20th century, and its influence is still felt today.

The book's success owes much to de Beauvoir's brilliant writing style and passion, but both are rooted in the clarity of her critical thinking skills. She builds a strong argument against the silent assumptions that continually demoted (and still demote) women to "second place" in a society dominated by men. De Beauvoir also demonstrates the central skills of reasoning at their best: presenting a persuasive case, organising her thoughts, and supporting her conclusions.

Above all though, *The Second Sex* is a masterclass in analysis. Treating the structures of contemporary society and culture as a series of arguments that tend continuously to demote women, de Beauvoir is able to isolate and describe the implicit assumptions that underpin male domination. Her demolition of these assumptions provides the crucial ammunition for her argument that women are in no way the "second" sex, but are in every way the equal of men.

《世界思想宝库钥匙丛书》简介

《世界思想宝库钥匙丛书》致力于为一系列在各领域产生重大影响的人文社科类经典著作提供独特的学术探讨。每一本读物都不仅仅是原经典著作的内容摘要，而是介绍并深入研究原经典著作的学术渊源、主要观点和历史影响。这一丛书的目的是提供一套学习资料，以促进读者掌握批判性思维，从而更全面、深刻地去理解重要思想。

每一本读物分为 3 个部分：学术渊源、学术思想和学术影响，每个部分下有 4 个小节。这些章节旨在从各个方面研究原经典著作及其反响。

由于独特的体例，每一本读物不但易于阅读，而且另有一项优点：所有读物的编排体例相同，读者在进行某个知识层面的调查或研究时可交叉参阅多本该丛书中的相关读物，从而开启跨领域研究的路径。

为了方便阅读，每本读物最后还列出了术语表和人名表（在书中则以星号 * 标记），此外还有参考文献。

《世界思想宝库钥匙丛书》与剑桥大学合作，理清了批判性思维的要点，即如何通过 6 种技能来进行有效思考。其中 3 种技能让我们能够理解问题，另 3 种技能让我们有能力解决问题。这 6 种技能合称为"批判性思维 PACIER 模式"，它们是：

分析：了解如何建立一个观点；
评估：研究一个观点的优点和缺点；
阐释：对意义所产生的问题加以理解；
创造性思维：提出新的见解，发现新的联系；
解决问题：提出切实有效的解决办法；
理性化思维：创建有说服力的观点。

THE MACAT LIBRARY

The Macat Library is a series of unique academic explorations of seminal works in the humanities and social sciences — books and papers that have had a significant and widely recognised impact on their disciplines. It has been created to serve as much more than just a summary of what lies between the covers of a great book. It illuminates and explores the influences on, ideas of, and impact of that book. Our goal is to offer a learning resource that encourages critical thinking and fosters a better, deeper understanding of important ideas.

Each publication is divided into three Sections: Influences, Ideas, and Impact. Each Section has four Modules. These explore every important facet of the work, and the responses to it.

This Section-Module structure makes a Macat Library book easy to use, but it has another important feature. Because each Macat book is written to the same format, it is possible (and encouraged!) to cross-reference multiple Macat books along the same lines of inquiry or research. This allows the reader to open up interesting interdisciplinary pathways.

To further aid your reading, lists of glossary terms and people mentioned are included at the end of this book (these are indicated by an asterisk [*] throughout) — as well as a list of works cited.

Macat has worked with the University of Cambridge to identify the elements of critical thinking and understand the ways in which six different skills combine to enable effective thinking.

Three allow us to fully understand a problem; three more give us the tools to solve it. Together, these six skills make up the PACIER model of critical thinking. They are:

ANALYSIS — understanding how an argument is built
EVALUATION — exploring the strengths and weaknesses of an argument
INTERPRETATION — understanding issues of meaning
CREATIVE THINKING — coming up with new ideas and fresh connections
PROBLEM-SOLVING — producing strong solutions
REASONING — creating strong arguments

"《世界思想宝库钥匙丛书》提供了独一无二的跨学科学习和研究工具。它介绍那些革新了各自学科研究的经典著作，还邀请全世界一流专家和教育机构进行严谨的分析，为每位读者打开世界顶级教育的大门。"

—— 安德烈亚斯·施莱歇尔，
经济合作与发展组织教育与技能司司长

"《世界思想宝库钥匙丛书》直面大学教育的巨大挑战……他们组建了一支精干而活跃的学者队伍，来推出在研究广度上颇具新意的教学材料。"

—— 布罗尔斯教授、勋爵，剑桥大学前校长

"《世界思想宝库钥匙丛书》的愿景令人赞叹。它通过分析和阐释那些曾深刻影响人类思想以及社会、经济发展的经典文本，提供了新的学习方法。它推动批判性思维，这对于任何社会和经济体来说都是至关重要的。这就是未来的学习方法。"

—— 查尔斯·克拉克阁下，英国前教育大臣

"对于那些影响了各自领域的著作，《世界思想宝库钥匙丛书》能让人们立即了解到围绕那些著作展开的评论性言论，这让该系列图书成为在这些领域从事研究的师生们不可或缺的资源。"

—— 威廉·特朗佐教授，加利福尼亚大学圣地亚哥分校

"Macat offers an amazing first-of-its-kind tool for interdisciplinary learning and research. Its focus on works that transformed their disciplines and its rigorous approach, drawing on the world's leading experts and educational institutions, opens up a world-class education to anyone."

—— Andreas Schleicher, Director for Education and Skills, Organisation for Economic Co-operation and Development

"Macat is taking on some of the major challenges in university education... They have drawn together a strong team of active academics who are producing teaching materials that are novel in the breadth of their approach."

—— Prof Lord Broers, former Vice-Chancellor of the University of Cambridge

"The Macat vision is exceptionally exciting. It focuses upon new modes of learning which analyse and explain seminal texts which have profoundly influenced world thinking and so social and economic development. It promotes the kind of critical thinking which is essential for any society and economy. This is the learning of the future."

—— Rt Hon Charles Clarke, former UK Secretary of State for Education

"The Macat analyses provide immediate access to the critical conversation surrounding the books that have shaped their respective discipline, which will make them an invaluable resource to all of those, students and teachers, working in the field."

—— Prof William Tronzo, University of California at San Diego

TITLE	中文书名	类别
An Analysis of Arjun Appadurai's *Modernity at Large: Cultural Dimensions of Globalization*	解析阿尔君·阿帕杜莱《消失的现代性：全球化的文化维度》	人类学
An Analysis of Claude Lévi-Strauss's *Structural Anthropology*	解析克劳德·列维-施特劳斯《结构人类学》	人类学
An Analysis of Marcel Mauss's *The Gift*	解析马塞尔·莫斯《礼物》	人类学
An Analysis of Jared M. Diamond's *Guns, Germs, and Steel: The Fate of Human Societies*	解析贾雷德·M.戴蒙德《枪炮、病菌与钢铁：人类社会的命运》	人类学
An Analysis of Clifford Geertz's *The Interpretation of Cultures*	解析克利福德·格尔茨《文化的解释》	人类学
An Analysis of Philippe Ariès's *Centuries of Childhood: A Social History of Family Life*	解析菲力浦·阿利埃斯《儿童的世纪：旧制度下的儿童和家庭生活》	人类学
An Analysis of W. Chan Kim & Renée Mauborgne's *Blue Ocean Strategy*	解析金伟灿/勒妮·莫博涅《蓝海战略》	商业
An Analysis of John P. Kotter's *Leading Change*	解析约翰·P.科特《领导变革》	商业
An Analysis of Michael E. Porter's *Competitive Strategy: Techniques for Analyzing Industries and Competitors*	解析迈克尔·E.波特《竞争战略：分析产业和竞争对手的技术》	商业
An Analysis of Jean Lave & Etienne Wenger's *Situated Learning: Legitimate Peripheral Participation*	解析琼·莱夫/艾蒂纳·温格《情境学习：合法的边缘性参与》	商业
An Analysis of Douglas McGregor's *The Human Side of Enterprise*	解析道格拉斯·麦格雷戈《企业的人性面》	商业
An Analysis of Milton Friedman's *Capitalism and Freedom*	解析米尔顿·弗里德曼《资本主义与自由》	商业
An Analysis of Ludwig von Mises's *The Theory of Money and Credit*	解析路德维希·冯·米塞斯《货币和信用理论》	经济学
An Analysis of Adam Smith's *The Wealth of Nations*	解析亚当·斯密《国富论》	经济学
An Analysis of Thomas Piketty's *Capital in the Twenty-First Century*	解析托马斯·皮凯蒂《21世纪资本论》	经济学
An Analysis of Nassim Nicholas Taleb's *The Black Swan: The Impact of the Highly Improbable*	解析纳西姆·尼古拉斯·塔勒布《黑天鹅：如何应对不可预知的未来》	经济学
An Analysis of Ha-Joon Chang's *Kicking Away the Ladder*	解析张夏准《富国陷阱：发达国家为何踢开梯子》	经济学
An Analysis of Thomas Robert Malthus's *An Essay on the Principle of Population*	解析托马斯·罗伯特·马尔萨斯《人口论》	经济学

An Analysis of John Maynard Keynes's *The General Theory of Employment, Interest and Money*	解析约翰·梅纳德·凯恩斯《就业、利息和货币通论》	经济学
An Analysis of Milton Friedman's *The Role of Monetary Policy*	解析米尔顿·弗里德曼《货币政策的作用》	经济学
An Analysis of Burton G. Malkiel's *A Random Walk Down Wall Street*	解析伯顿·G.马尔基尔《漫步华尔街》	经济学
An Analysis of Friedrich A. Hayek's *The Road to Serfdom*	解析弗里德里希·A.哈耶克《通往奴役之路》	经济学
An Analysis of Charles P. Kindleberger's *Manias, Panics, and Crashes: A History of Financial Crises*	解析查尔斯·P.金德尔伯格《疯狂、惊恐和崩溃：金融危机史》	经济学
An Analysis of Amartya Sen's *Development as Freedom*	解析阿马蒂亚·森《以自由看待发展》	经济学
An Analysis of Rachel Carson's *Silent Spring*	解析蕾切尔·卡森《寂静的春天》	地理学
An Analysis of Charles Darwin's *On the Origin of Species: by Means of Natural Selection, or The Preservation of Favoured Races in the Struggle for Life*	解析查尔斯·达尔文《物种起源》	地理学
An Analysis of World Commission on Environment and Development's *The Brundtland Report, Our Common Future*	解析世界环境与发展委员会《布伦特兰报告：我们共同的未来》	地理学
An Analysis of James E. Lovelock's *Gaia: A New Look at Life on Earth*	解析詹姆斯·E.拉伍洛克《盖娅：地球生命的新视野》	地理学
An Analysis of Paul Kennedy's *The Rise and Fall of the Great Powers: Economic Change and Military Conflict from 1500—2000*	解析保罗·肯尼迪《大国的兴衰：1500—2000年的经济变革与军事冲突》	历史
An Analysis of Janet L. Abu-Lughod's *Before European Hegemony: The World System A. D. 1250—1350*	解析珍妮特·L.阿布-卢格霍德《欧洲霸权之前：1250—1350年的世界体系》	历史
An Analysis of Alfred W. Crosby's *The Columbian Exchange: Biological and Cultural Consequences of 1492*	解析艾尔弗雷德·W.克罗斯比《哥伦布大交换：1492年以后的生物影响和文化冲击》	历史
An Analysis of Tony Judt's *Postwar: A History of Europe since 1945*	解析托尼·朱特《战后欧洲史》	历史
An Analysis of Richard J. Evans's *In Defence of History*	解析理查德·J.艾文斯《捍卫历史》	历史
An Analysis of Eric Hobsbawm's *The Age of Revolution: Europe 1789–1848*	解析艾瑞克·霍布斯鲍姆《革命的年代：欧洲1789—1848年》	历史

An Analysis of Roland Barthes's *Mythologies*	解析罗兰·巴特《神话学》	文学与批判理论
An Analysis of Simone de Beauvoir's *The Second Sex*	解析西蒙娜·德·波伏娃《第二性》	文学与批判理论
An Analysis of Edward W. Said's *Orientalism*	解析爱德华·W.萨义德《东方主义》	文学与批判理论
An Analysis of Virginia Woolf's *A Room of One's Own*	解析弗吉尼亚·伍尔芙《一间自己的房间》	文学与批判理论
An Analysis of Judith Butler's *Gender Trouble*	解析朱迪斯·巴特勒《性别麻烦》	文学与批判理论
An Analysis of Ferdinand de Saussure's *Course in General Linguistics*	解析费尔迪南·德·索绪尔《普通语言学教程》	文学与批判理论
An Analysis of Susan Sontag's *On Photography*	解析苏珊·桑塔格《论摄影》	文学与批判理论
An Analysis of Walter Benjamin's *The Work of Art in the Age of Mechanical Reproduction*	解析瓦尔特·本雅明《机械复制时代的艺术作品》	文学与批判理论
An Analysis of W.E.B. Du Bois's *The Souls of Black Folk*	解析 W.E.B. 杜波依斯《黑人的灵魂》	文学与批判理论
An Analysis of Plato's *The Republic*	解析柏拉图《理想国》	哲学
An Analysis of Plato's *Symposium*	解析柏拉图《会饮篇》	哲学
An Analysis of Aristotle's *Metaphysics*	解析亚里士多德《形而上学》	哲学
An Analysis of Aristotle's *Nicomachean Ethics*	解析亚里士多德《尼各马可伦理学》	哲学
An Analysis of Immanuel Kant's *Critique of Pure Reason*	解析伊曼努尔·康德《纯粹理性批判》	哲学
An Analysis of Ludwig Wittgenstein's *Philosophical Investigations*	解析路德维希·维特根斯坦《哲学研究》	哲学
An Analysis of G.W.F. Hegel's *Phenomenology of Spirit*	解析 G.W.F. 黑格尔《精神现象学》	哲学
An Analysis of Baruch Spinoza's *Ethics*	解析巴鲁赫·斯宾诺莎《伦理学》	哲学
An Analysis of Hannah Arendt's *The Human Condition*	解析汉娜·阿伦特《人的境况》	哲学
An Analysis of G.E.M. Anscombe's *Modern Moral Philosophy*	解析 G.E.M. 安斯康姆《现代道德哲学》	哲学
An Analysis of David Hume's *An Enquiry Concerning Human Understanding*	解析大卫·休谟《人类理解研究》	哲学

An Analysis of Søren Kierkegaard's *Fear and Trembling*	解析索伦·克尔凯郭尔《恐惧与战栗》	哲学
An Analysis of René Descartes's *Meditations on First Philosophy*	解析勒内·笛卡尔《第一哲学沉思录》	哲学
An Analysis of Friedrich Nietzsche's *On the Genealogy of Morality*	解析弗里德里希·尼采《论道德的谱系》	哲学
An Analysis of Gilbert Ryle's *The Concept of Mind*	解析吉尔伯特·赖尔《心的概念》	哲学
An Analysis of Thomas Kuhn's *The Structure of Scientific Revolutions*	解析托马斯·库恩《科学革命的结构》	哲学
An Analysis of John Stuart Mill's *Utilitarianism*	解析约翰·斯图亚特·穆勒《功利主义》	哲学
An Analysis of Aristotle's *Politics*	解析亚里士多德《政治学》	政治学
An Analysis of Niccolò Machiavelli's *The Prince*	解析尼科洛·马基雅维利《君主论》	政治学
An Analysis of Karl Marx's *Capital*	解析卡尔·马克思《资本论》	政治学
An Analysis of Benedict Anderson's *Imagined Communities*	解析本尼迪克特·安德森《想象的共同体》	政治学
An Analysis of Samuel P. Huntington's *The Clash of Civilizations and the Remaking of World Order*	解析塞缪尔·P.亨廷顿《文明的冲突与世界秩序的重建》	政治学
An Analysis of Alexis de Tocqueville's *Democracy in America*	解析阿列克西·德·托克维尔《论美国的民主》	政治学
An Analysis of John A. Hobson's *Imperialism: A Study*	解析约翰·A.霍布森《帝国主义》	政治学
An Analysis of Thomas Paine's *Common Sense*	解析托马斯·潘恩《常识》	政治学
An Analysis of John Rawls's *A Theory of Justice*	解析约翰·罗尔斯《正义论》	政治学
An Analysis of Francis Fukuyama's *The End of History and the Last Man*	解析弗朗西斯·福山《历史的终结与最后的人》	政治学
An Analysis of John Locke's *Two Treatises of Government*	解析约翰·洛克《政府论》	政治学
An Analysis of Sun Tzu's *The Art of War*	解析孙武《孙子兵法》	政治学
An Analysis of Henry Kissinger's *World Order: Reflections on the Character of Nations and the Course of History*	解析亨利·基辛格《世界秩序》	政治学
An Analysis of Jean-Jacques Rousseau's *The Social Contract*	解析让-雅克·卢梭《社会契约论》	政治学

An Analysis of Odd Arne Westad's *The Global Cold War: Third World Interventions and the Making of Our Times*	解析文安立《全球冷战：美苏对第三世界的干涉与当代世界的形成》	政治学
An Analysis of Sigmund Freud's *The Interpretation of Dreams*	解析西格蒙德·弗洛伊德《梦的解析》	心理学
An Analysis of William James' *The Principles of Psychology*	解析威廉·詹姆斯《心理学原理》	心理学
An Analysis of Philip Zimbardo's *The Lucifer Effect*	解析菲利普·津巴多《路西法效应》	心理学
An Analysis of Leon Festinger's *A Theory of Cognitive Dissonance*	解析利昂·费斯汀格《认知失调论》	心理学
An Analysis of Richard H. Thaler & Cass R. Sunstein's *Nudge: Improving Decisions about Health, Wealth, and Happiness*	解析理查德·H.泰勒／卡斯·R.桑斯坦《助推：如何做出有关健康、财富和幸福的更优决策》	心理学
An Analysis of Gordon Allport's *The Nature of Prejudice*	解析高尔登·奥尔波特《偏见的本质》	心理学
An Analysis of Steven Pinker's *The Better Angels of Our Nature: Why Violence Has Declined*	解析斯蒂芬·平克《人性中的善良天使：暴力为什么会减少》	心理学
An Analysis of Stanley Milgram's *Obedience to Authority*	解析斯坦利·米尔格拉姆《对权威的服从》	心理学
An Analysis of Betty Friedan's *The Feminine Mystique*	解析贝蒂·弗里丹《女性的奥秘》	心理学
An Analysis of David Riesman's *The Lonely Crowd: A Study of the Changing American Character*	解析大卫·理斯曼《孤独的人群：美国人社会性格演变之研究》	社会学
An Analysis of Franz Boas's *Race, Language and Culture*	解析弗朗兹·博厄斯《种族、语言与文化》	社会学
An Analysis of Pierre Bourdieu's *Outline of a Theory of Practice*	解析皮埃尔·布尔迪厄《实践理论大纲》	社会学
An Analysis of Max Weber's *The Protestant Ethic and the Spirit of Capitalism*	解析马克斯·韦伯《新教伦理与资本主义精神》	社会学
An Analysis of Jane Jacobs's *The Death and Life of Great American Cities*	解析简·雅各布斯《美国大城市的死与生》	社会学
An Analysis of C. Wright Mills's *The Sociological Imagination*	解析C.赖特·米尔斯《社会学的想象力》	社会学
An Analysis of Robert E. Lucas Jr.'s *Why Doesn't Capital Flow from Rich to Poor Countries?*	解析小罗伯特·E.卢卡斯《为何资本不从富国流向穷国？》	社会学

An Analysis of Émile Durkheim's *On Suicide*	解析埃米尔·迪尔凯姆《自杀论》	社会学
An Analysis of Eric Hoffer's *The True Believer: Thoughts on the Nature of Mass Movements*	解析埃里克·霍弗《狂热分子：群众运动圣经》	社会学
An Analysis of Jared M. Diamond's *Collapse: How Societies Choose to Fail or Survive*	解析贾雷德·M.戴蒙德《大崩溃：社会如何选择兴亡》	社会学
An Analysis of Michel Foucault's *The History of Sexuality Vol. 1: The Will to Knowledge*	解析米歇尔·福柯《性史（第一卷）:求知意志》	社会学
An Analysis of Michel Foucault's *Discipline and Punish*	解析米歇尔·福柯《规训与惩罚》	社会学
An Analysis of Richard Dawkins's *The Selfish Gene*	解析理查德·道金斯《自私的基因》	社会学
An Analysis of Antonio Gramsci's *Prison Notebooks*	解析安东尼奥·葛兰西《狱中札记》	社会学
An Analysis of Augustine's *Confessions*	解析奥古斯丁《忏悔录》	神学
An Analysis of C. S. Lewis's *The Abolition of Man*	解析 C. S. 路易斯《人之废》	神学

图书在版编目（CIP）数据

解析西蒙娜·德·波伏娃《第二性》：汉、英 / 拉凯莱·迪尼（Rachele Dini）著；
杨建玫译. —上海：上海外语教育出版社，2020
（世界思想宝库钥匙丛书）
ISBN 978-7-5446-6121-8

Ⅰ.①解… Ⅱ.①拉… ②杨… Ⅲ.①波伏瓦(Beauvoir, Simone de 1908－1986)－
妇女问题－思想评论－汉、英 Ⅳ.①B565.59

中国版本图书馆CIP数据核字（2020）第014369号

This Chinese-English bilingual edition of *An Analysis of Simone de Beauvoir's The Second Sex*
is published by arrangement with MACAT International Limited.
Licensed for sale throughout the world.

本书汉英双语版由Macat国际有限公司授权上海外语教育出版社有限公司出版。
供在全世界范围内发行、销售。

图字：09－2018－549

出版发行：**上海外语教育出版社**
（上海外国语大学内）　邮编：200083
电　　话：021-65425300（总机）
电子邮箱：bookinfo@sflep.com.cn
网　　址：http://www.sflep.com
责任编辑：梁瀚杰

印　　刷：上海宝山译文印刷厂
开　　本：890×1240　1/32　印张 6.375　字数 130千字
版　　次：2020年5月第1版　2020年5月第1次印刷
印　　数：2 100 册

书　　号：ISBN 978-7-5446-6121-8
定　　价：30.00 元

本版图书如有印装质量问题，可向本社调换
质量服务热线：4008-213-263　电子邮箱：editorial@sflep.com